DO IT!

EVERY SOUTH AFRICAN'S GUIDE TO
MAKING A DIFFERENCE

JAMES MOTLATSI AND BOBBY GODSELL

JACANA

First published by Jacana Media (Pty) Ltd in 2008

10 Orange Street
Sunnyside
Auckland Park 2092
South Africa
+2711 628 3200
www.jacana.co.za

ISBN 978-1-77009-640-0

Cover design by Trevor Paul
Set in Stempel Garamond 11/16pt
Printed by CTP Book Printers, Cape Town
Job No. 000862

See a complete list of Jacana titles at www.jacana.co.za

I want to thank the following people, my wife Mapula Matumelo Motlatsi for her support; Dillo Mashale; Rats'iu Majara; Janet Dannhauser the Executive Secretary, for her patient willingess to rearrange my appointments at the last minute to enable me to work on this book; Teba Executive and Teba Management for giving me time to complete this project; and all those people who assisted me.

JAMES MOTLATSI

'To my parents who taught me about good values, and my wife Gillian and daughters Megan, Sarah and Abigail who have shown me how to live them.'

BOBBY GODSELL

CONTENTS

WHY WE WROTE THIS BOOK

A RELATIONSHIP FORGED IN TOUGH TIMES, AND TESTED BY BIG CHALLENGES

This book was born out of the relationship between James Motlatsi, founding President of the National Union of Mineworkers (NUM), now Executive Chair of Teba, and Bobby Godsell, founder CEO of AngloGoldAshanti, long-time labour negotiator in the mining industry and now happy pensioner, though also a brave one, having just become non-executive Chair of Eskom.

Our relationship grew out of a climate of deep mistrust, violence and bitter conflict. It has survived some pretty big setbacks and both of us have mastered some important challenges.

The relationship is certainly historically unusual though in no way unique. As the two of us reflected on our country's current state, it seemed to us that what we had learnt together, and indeed what we had done together, had something to say about the leadership that ordinary South Africans like ourselves could display, and need to display.

We could hardly be more different South Africans: by race, class, language (and tribe!). Marcel Golding,

1

former Deputy General Secretary of the National Union of Mineworkers, used to point out that what you see of a mountain depends on where you are standing on it. We clearly stand in two very different places. However, over two decades we have discovered some very potent shared interests and common loyalties.

We also share an impatience with established authority and an unwillingness to wait for others to do things for us, or to tell us what to do. We are active citizens! And we call upon you to join us!

It is by seeing our shared interests and common loyalties, and by having the willingness to act upon that knowledge, that we and you will take our nation forward.

This book is largely about the responsibilities of citizens: in the home, the school, the workplace, and the community, and in the public marketplace of ideas. Few laws reach effectively into these social spaces, and quite often the citizen is the authority in these places. The wisest, most progressive and sensible laws and policies and the best-run government departments require the actions of citizens to achieve results.

In this book we look at what the citizen can do as co-architect of a peaceful, prosperous and democratic South Africa in the areas of crime, corruption, education, poverty and debt. In each of these areas we discuss both the ideas and the actions that should be the markers of a good citizen.

Ideas are an expression of beliefs and values. These beliefs and values frame our actions. They provide the context in which we construct the choices between acting in this way or that.

Action without ideas is dangerous. Without action, however, ideas, values and beliefs are useless.

But first see where we have come from.

JAMES MOTLATSI:
WHAT I KNOW ABOUT BOBBY GODSELL

Our relationship started in 1987 immediately after the great mineworkers' strike. I still recall that when we were negotiating we received a message that on the President Steyn gold mine (now Bambanani) mine security was using tear gas and rubber bullets against the striking workers. I remember Cyril Ramaphosa showing a tear gas canister and saying, 'Baas Godsell, what is this?'

The negotiations were difficult and it took a long time to reach agreement. Of particular importance and as a direct result of these negotiations was the finalisation of a Code of Conduct. Remember also that during that time I was banned from the Anglo American mines.

In early 1990 after the departure of Cyril from NUM, I was tasked to take over some of the work that he had previously done. This whilst our areas of responsibility were clear and very different. I now had to become involved with both direct and indirect negotiations.

In 1992 we took a trip to Germany with the mining industry. Our team comprised myself, Jerry Majatladi and Marcel Golding whilst Bobby headed up the industry team. The intention was to try and understand the concept of co-determination – a German system of company management with union representatives on company boards – but, to be honest, we did not trust each other at the beginning of the trip. However, the Germans placed us on a very tight schedule and we had no option but to join forces and work together. We then continued to Belgium where we were supposed to address the European Union. This was the first address that I made in conjunction with and on the same platform as an employer body.

We agreed with Bobby that the model developed from this trip was the right one and we then invited the Germans to South Africa to see the model in action. The Chamber of Mines was not interested. Bobby did not tell me that he had failed to convince the Chamber of Mines. I was told by a source in the Chamber that when Bobby and his team reported back to the Chamber they were accused of trying to have the mining industry adopt some type of 'communist practice'.

On 10 April 1993 I received a call that Chris Hani had been murdered. I immediately rushed to the scene and found Tokyo Sexwale and Sam Shilowa there. We agreed that we needed to have a Tripartite Alliance meeting immediately and we met that same evening at the ANC head office known then as Shell House (now Albert Luthuli House). The tensions were so high that we decided to adjourn the meeting and continue the following day. The next day it was decided that I should head up a committee to co-ordinate the funeral arrangements. Immediately after the meeting I went to those in authority, who told me that it was not ANC policy to use organisational funds to bury members – regardless of their status – when they passed away.

I subsequently approached all Cosatu affiliates for donations but could only raise an amount of R76,000. I called Bobby and told him that there was a national crisis and we needed money to bury Chris Hani.

In no time he phoned me and told me that the Chamber of Mines has approved a donation of R450,000 but we needed to open a separate account because they did not want to be seen as supporting political parties. He also told me that he had already spoken to Coca-Cola, Premier Milling and City Funerals, to obtain their assistance. Following our meetings all of them agreed to support us. It was after all this that my attitude changed towards Bobby. It must be made clear that Bobby, in his capacity as President of the Chamber of Mines, and I, as President of the National Union of Mineworkers, were effectively natural enemies simply because of our respective positions.

At the 1994 NUM congress it was resolved that union representatives should sit on the boards of directors of the various mining houses if so invited. Gwede Mantashe was the first member of the executive to sit on the board of Samancor, the South African

Manganese Corporation, and was followed by Kgalema Motlanthe on the board of Rand Mutual Assurance.

AngloGold invited me to join their board in 1996 but the union's executive was not happy with this, and the issue continued to be discussed within NUM for some eighteen months. It was finally approved and I became a board member of AngloGold, but on condition that my appointment would not be reported in the media. This proved to be completely impractical as my appointment was widely known within days if not hours.

During 1998 I was part of the AngloGold delegation that travelled to London and New York to facilitate the listing of AngloGold on those stock exchanges. I received a hostile reception in New York because NUM members had just burnt sections of Megawatt Park back in Johannesburg. I was asked why I should want investors in the United Kingdom and United States to invest in the South African mining industry when our union's members were destroying buildings and property. My response was a simple one and this was that unfortunately every organisation has some undisciplined members and that the union would take the necessary action against them.

In 1999 Britain decided to sell some of its gold reserves and the International Monetary Fund (IMF) then followed suit. This ultimately caused the gold price to drop to US$250 an ounce. To prevent any further selling by certain governments, Bobby suggested that the NUM and the Chamber of Mines travel jointly to the United States to persuade the US government not to support the sale of gold by the IMF. If we had failed in our quest it would have meant the probable retrenchment of some 85,000 mineworkers in the gold-mining industry.

I, as the President of NUM, and Bobby, as President of the Chamber of Mines, undertook the journey to the USA where we were successful in convincing the Black Caucus, Republican Senators and other legislators not to support such sales.

Our second trip was to the United Kingdom where we met with the Labour Party government. Here we had much less success. I recall being invited to a Trades Union Congress function where the then Chancellor of the Exchequer, Gordon Brown, was introduced to me. He then left the function without any further discussion with me, nor did he attempt to explain the reason for his decision. Our third trip was to Switzerland, which was very successful. At the end of our visit we organised a joint march to the offices of the British High Commission. This was the first march of its kind where both employers and employees marched under the joint banners of the National Union of Mineworkers and the Chamber of Mines. Many people criticised us by asking what impact our march could possibly have on the gold price. To our absolute delight and their chagrin, the price of gold increased by more than $100 after the march.

The direct consequence of this was the fact that no mineworker lost his or her job, as originally feared. A second benefit was the fact that both Bobby and I were now able to transcend our fundamental differences and work together, although we also agreed to disagree on certain points! We fully agreed that the South African mining industry was a national asset that needed to be protected by all concerned. It was not simply for either employers or employees.

BOBBY GODSELL:
WHAT I HAVE LEARNT ABOUT JAMES MOTLATSI

My earliest memory of James Motlatsi is the way in which in an early 1980s encounter he put on his jacket, stood up and marched out of a small group negotiation with unbelievable speed. One moment everything was calm and orderly. The next moment the meeting was over and had ended in anger, expressed both in words and in body language.

The next memory is of the anger of my colleague, Peter Gush, then Chairman of Anglo's Gold Division, when James, during the 1987 strike, stood in front of the shaft head gear at the Western Deep Levels mine and said, 'If I have to tear down this mine brick by brick to end apartheid, that is just what I am going to do.' 'Fire that man,' said Gush.

He was fired. The reason? For going on strike when he was not in a recognised bargaining unit. I later joked that NUM really needed him as full-time President. Since James all union presidents (and many other union leaders) are 'released' from their jobs to do union work, but are still paid by the company. The current President has his salary paid by AngloGoldAshanti in terms of this policy.

Gush's response was ironic, as he too wanted apartheid to end. But the strike was not about ending a political system; it was a battle for control of the mines. Subsequently Motlatsi and Gush became good friends, and worked together when Peter ran the De Beers mines.

The low gold price produced a crisis. Workers wanted wage increases. Higher costs would limit the extent of ore reserves that could be mined profitably and thereby shorten the life of the mine, causing workers to lose their jobs. How to escape this bad trade-off? If we could produce enough additional gold to cover the cost of the wage increase, we could mine the same amount of gold and keep current employment levels. At AngloGold we needed to produce an extra 10 tonnes of gold, or about 10 per cent more each year. That's the deal AngloGoldAshanti and NUM made, and it worked for both of us for the two years it lasted.

The very low gold price was mainly the result of the threat of the massive sale of gold held in the inventories of many developed countries' Central Banks, as well as by international institutions such as the International Monetary Fund. This gold, obtained mainly in periods of colonial conquest, was held on the books of many Central Banks at very low cost, making the banks insensitive sellers. At the head of the selling queue were the Bank of England, the International Monetary Fund and the Swiss National Bank. The IMF needed the support of the US government in order to sell. The US government in turn needed a resolution to be passed in the US Congress before it could support such a sale. So James and I, as the President of NUM and the President of the Chamber of Mines, set out to lobby Congress. We found right-wing Republicans who opposed the IMF as an international money plot, and left-wing Democrats who disliked IMF structural adjustment programmes, more than ready to listen to us. When we met the Black Caucus James's credentials were obvious. Fortunately for me, a member of the caucus had heard of me from a leading New York unionist, Victor Gotbaum, who had become a good friend. They read a resolution on our 'cause' into the Congressional Record. It was clear Congressional support would require major work, and probably important political concessions from the Federal Administration. The IMF decided against sales.

Our trip to London was much less successful. It seemed that much of British society knew how to talk either to black or to white South Africans, but not to a joint delegation! When James told a BBC interviewer that the then Chancellor of the Exchequer, now Prime Minister Gordon Brown, was a coward, it made me a very proud African.

The World Economic Forum holds regular private meetings of Central Bankers. In 1998 they invited the new South African President, Thabo Mbeki, to address the meeting. President Mbeki's office turned down the invitation, even though he would be at the annual WEF meeting in Davos. Motlatsi arranged for the two of us to go and see the President on a Saturday morning. He was aware neither of the invite, nor that it had been declined on his behalf. He attended the meeting (as did James and myself) and spoke brilliantly about the impact of reckless sales on emerging-market gold producers.

Not all of our attempts at political influence were as successful as this!

Subsequently the Central Banks agreed amongst themselves to limit and co-ordinate both the selling and lending of gold. The gold price started to rise.

When James agreed to become a director of the newly created AngloGold, we wanted to launch this company with the mother of all parties. We hired the Coca-Cola Dome in Johannesburg, and invited 5,000 people, mainly from the company's mines in South Africa and Mali. In the week before this launch, angry NUM protesters, involved in a wage dispute, set fire to part of an Eskom college. Management was understandably nervous. James was calm. We had a great party.

When we listed the company on the New York stock exchange, we took a lion onto the trading floor. James positioned himself furthest from the lion. 'I am the only black man around,' he quipped. 'He'll eat me first.'

Motlatsi is generally a man of few words. He asks tough questions. His loyalty is to values and not blindly to people. I have benefited from tough criticism and tough questions. It is possible to be chastised by someone who has so clearly demonstrated his deep loyalty to the industry whose future he helped shape, and to the country which has become his home.

A NATION UNDER CONSTRUCTION

IDEAS:

WHO ARE WE?

In 1941 the journalist G.H. Calpin wrote a book entitled *There are no South Africans*. The book is almost exclusively about white South African politics. Here are the opening words: 'The worst of South Africa is that you never come across a South African. There is no surprise in the discovery that the United States produces Americans; or China, Chinese; or Lapland, Laplanders. The naturalness of so natural a condition does not strike one until its exception appears. The exception is South Africa.'[1]

In 1958 Nadine Gordimer penned her second novel, *A world of strangers*.[2] The novel describes the two, almost completely separate worlds of white and black South Africa under high apartheid.

In 1996 President Thabo Mbeki made a speech to mark the adoption of South Africa's new constitution entitled 'I am an African'.[3]

Mbeki's speech, surely his most remarkable, sets out in poetic terms the identity quilt from which we must forge a common citizenry.

'I owe my being to the Khoi and the San whose

13

desolate souls haunt the great expanses of the beautiful Cape ... I am formed of the migrants who left Europe to find a new home on our native land ... In my veins courses the blood of the Malay slaves who came from the East ... I am the grandchild of the warrior men and women that Hintsa and Sekhukhune led, the patriots that Cetshwayo and Mphephu took to battle ... I am the grandchild who lays fresh flowers on the Boer grave at St Helena and the Bahamas, who sees in the mind's eye and suffers the suffering of a simple peasant folk, death, concentration camps, destroyed homesteads, a dream in ruins ... I am the child of Nongqawuse. I am he who made it possible to trade in the world markets in diamonds, in gold, in the same food for which my stomach yearns ... I come of those who were transported from India and China, whose being resided in the fact, solely, that they were able to provide physical labour ... I am an African!'

All three examples cited above focus on the single, central question that continues to confront our still very young nation. Who are we?

Our new constitution is clear:

'[This constitution] is a firm assertion made by ourselves that South Africa belongs to all who live in it, black and white.'

But the lived reality of 48 million South Africans is more confused.

Let us remember the park benches that commanded 'Europeans only'. And indeed the icons of our previous nationhood are replete with echoes of our European past. The evidence is everywhere. Look at street names and the names of suburbs and even towns. English, Scottish and Irish counties, European flowers, European rivers and mountains abound.

It is hardly surprising that people should bring icons in their luggage on the small ships that transported them from a cold Europe to the hot southern tip of Africa. The problem is not the bringing. All immigrant people do this. The challenge is whether this symbolic suitcase becomes a prison of past associations or a bridge to new experience. An excellent example of cultural baggage as a bridge rather than a prison is to be found in the language Afrikaans. At some point the Dutch speakers who emigrated to South African shores decided not merely to modify idiom and accent but to create a new language. Although it clearly remains a derivative of Dutch, Afrikaans is also a language that found a new home in a new country. It has been shaped and enriched by that new country and by the new people the language encountered there. It is arguably the most widely understood language in our country (used and understood by some 10 million South Africans) and the only linguistic legacy of the vast Dutch empire of this early nation of explorers.

As Nicholas Ostler in his majestic book *Empires of the Word* noted, 'Curiously but significantly, it was only in Africa that (the Dutch) colonial intrusiveness bore any linguistic fruit ... Taking all [the South Africans], the 10 million who know the language compare significantly with the 20 million or so who now speak Dutch worldwide.⁴

The other language which originated in Europe, English, has also developed a distinctly South African character, and joins Indian and American English as a dialect in its own right.

As people crossed into the borders of our country, each brought a cultural suitcase, and each has made it part prison, part bridge.

This question of who we are is well captured by the common experience of white and black South Africans. Whites generally have no trouble as seeing themselves, and calling themselves, *South Africans*. Black South Africans often make use of a different identity, as did President Mbeki in his signal speech. They refer to themselves as Africans. When both black and white are equally comfortable with either identity we will know that our world is becoming less strange.

IDEAS:
TWO EXAMPLES OF
PATCHWORK QUILT COUNTRIES?

United States of America

Given the diversity of our origins and our often bloody history, we should hardly be surprised by our divided identities. However, if we are to realise the promise of our constitution, we cannot be satisfied with this state of affairs. There is much we can learn from a nation of a similar age to 'modern' South Africa, the United States of America.

'The peopling of America is one of the great dramas in all of human history. Over the years, a massive stream of humanity – 45 million people – crossed every ocean and continent to reach the United States. They came speaking every language and representing every nationality, race and religion. Today, there are more people of Irish ancestry in the United States than in Ireland, more Jews than in Israel, more blacks than in most African countries. There are more people of Polish ancestry in Detroit than in most of the leading cities in Poland, and more than twice as many people of Italian ancestry in New York as in Venice.'

Thus writes Thomas Sowell in his history, *Ethnic America*.[5]

With this immense diversity of peoples, histories, languages, religions and cultures, how did this nation achieve one of the strongest senses of national identity and common citizenship in history?

National identity does not exist as a kind of cultural DNA. It is a social construct. How well it has been constructed in the USA. The icons of what it means to be American are to be found everywhere. In every classroom in every school in the country, there is an American flag, and each school day for both student and teacher starts with the pledge of allegiance.

'I pledge allegiance to the United States of America, and to the Republic for which it stands, one nation under God, with liberty and justice for all.'

Most social gatherings will include the singing of the national anthem. This anthem does not belong to one race, language or religious group. It has no culture-specific significance. This is true for major public holidays. Independence Day belongs equally to all Americans. The major holiday weekend is Thanksgiving. This holiday owes its present timing to the great economic depression of the 1930s and the desire by President Roosevelt to encourage in effect an early start to Christmas shopping.

What is important about this is that group culture and national identity in the USA have been separated. Everyone claims some of each. White Americans have a cultural identity: Italian, German, Polish or Irish. African Americans, Hispanic Americans, Japanese Americans have retained their cultural identities without in any way endangering or bringing into question their nationality.

This strong, inclusive and hyphenated sense of national identity has been achieved in the course of a national history replete with conflict, violence, discrimination and inequality. The wars of conquest waged by the first white settlers against what are now somewhat confusingly known as Native Americans were as brutal, widespread and long-lived as the wars of conquest in our own country. The War of Independence divided white Americans. America's Civil War remains one of the world's most bloody conflicts.

'The number of soldiers who died between 1861 and 1865, an estimated 620,000, is approximately equal to the total American fatalities in the Revolution, the War of 1812, the Mexican War, the Spanish-American War, World War I, World War II, and the Korean War combined. The Civil War's rate of death, its incidence in comparison with the size of the American population, was six times that of World War II. A similar rate, about 2 percent, in the United States today would mean six million fatalities.'[6]

Race discrimination was legally enforced well into the 1960s. Comprehensive equal rights for black Americans were only federally enforced after the passage of the Civil Rights Act of 1964.

No doubt there are singularities of history that make elements of the US experience unique. However, the energy devoted to the creation of an inclusive concept of citizenship stands as a challenge to South Africans.

Lesotho

We do not have to go as far as America for an example of an effective nation crafted out of divergent clans and tribes. Moshoeshoe I, born around 1786, created the Basotho nation through bringing together different Sotho clans with Nguni refugees.

'The arrival at Thaba-Bosiu is viewed by historians as a turning point in the history of Lesotho ... While at Thaba-Bosiu, Moshoeshoe did all he could to establish friendly relations with his neighbours at home and in the region at large. At home, he used marriage alliances as an instrument of peace and harmony amongst his subjects ... He called the cannibals from the mountains, gave them land and cattle, encouraged them to abandon their old lifestyles and allowed them to live among his people. He did this against the will of the majority of his people, who wanted to kill them. He brought together refugee groups and fragments of ethnic groups scattered all over by the Difaqane wars, into one nation.'[7]

IDEAS:
SOME BUILDING BLOCKS OF SHARED IDENTITY

South Africans have started well with a flag (designed by an advertising agency) which in a very short period of time has captured the hearts and become an icon for the vast majority of each group of our people. We have a national anthem that combines four languages and two pieces of music. More and more South Africans are mastering all four verses.

The Minister of Education, Naledi Pandor, has proposed a Pledge of Allegiance for school children. But why only for school children? We have excellent material in the preamble to our constitution. 'We recognise the injustices of our past; honour those who suffered for justice and freedom; respect those who have worked to build and develop our country; and believe that South Africa belongs to all who live in it, united in diversity.'

And there is material for a second pledge, a 'call to action'.

'We commit ourselves as citizens to:
- Heal the division of the past;
- Lay the foundation for a democratic and open society;
- Improve the quality of life of all citizens;
- And build a united and democratic South Africa.'[8]

How would it be if South Africans came to learn this meaning of their citizenship in four (or eleven!) languages? Would it not be a good way to start each day, each meeting, each religious service, each sporting match with such a pledge?

And there is much useful work that could be done with the other icons of our nationality. Why not review our national holidays? A comprehensive review could ensure that holidays with significance for all major groups were celebrated, together with at least one day that can be owned and shared by everyone, such as Freedom Day, the day that commemorates our first democratic election.

With a national calendar that truly represented the nation, a responsibility would devolve on the leadership (political, cultural, religious) of each major population group to find ways to engage their people on this day.

And with just a little bit of imagination and leadership the issue of naming streets, towns, rivers, dams and mountains could be made a vital part of the creation of a strong, inclusive sense of national identity. Ours is a big country. There is much to be named and renamed. How many numbered streets and avenues are to be found confusing both postmen and -women and visitors? How many main streets? How many Rietfonteins? And surely the time has come to rid ourselves of some part of our colonial clothing? How much do the English county names resonate with English-speaking South Africans? And even in the new construction of cluster villages do we really need to borrow so heavily from the Tuscan hills or the French and Spanish Riviera?

What if a names commission was created out of distinguished South Africans, each with an impressive track record of leadership and achievement in sport, the arts, religion, business and labour (no politicians or maybe one or two very special retired ones). What if this commission were to consider, say every five years, a limited number of significant name changes? A pattern of ten or a dozen changes that collectively would include rather than alienate? And what if this commission in its more regular work produced a list of names, in different languages, that captured the history, spirit, beauty and diversity of our nation, and offered these to citizens, property developers, and municipalities as new names for a new nation?

IDEAS:
CITIZENSHIP FOR IMMIGRANTS

All of the ideas suggested above are directed at building a strong common national identity amongst those 48

Immigrants 'should be taught to queue'

NEWCOMERS to the UK should receive welcome packs telling them not to spit in the street and to queue in shops, a minister said yesterday.

The packs would also urge them not to play music too loudly, not to touch people without permission and not to litter, according to Communities Secretary Hazel Blears.

Local councils should provide the information packs to help immigrants better integrate into British society, Blears said. — *Reuters*

million people who claim South African citizenship. But our country has in the past been a land of immigrants, and there is every indication that this will continue. For many nationals from elsewhere on our continent, but also from well beyond the shores of Africa, this country offers very attractive opportunities. Does this influx of people represent a threat or an opportunity? This turns exactly on how new entrants are received and how they behave. A process of making explicit the expectations of new citizens, and testing their willingness to accept both the responsibilities and rights of citizenship, would chart a clear path to an in-migration of people that will help build our nation. Making clear the expectations of citizenship, and making it possible for newcomers to accept these responsibilities, is the most meaningful response to the widespread climate of xenophobia.

Many countries are already applying citizenship tests to newcomers. Others are preparing to do so. Some proposed tests seem both superficial and unlikely to succeed.

High hopes, possible dreams

President Mbeki, in the same speech we quoted at the start of this chapter, expressed his hopes for our new constitution. Some of these hopes are worth recording in this context.

'The constitution whose adoption we celebrate constitutes an unequivocal statement that we refuse to accept that our Africanness shall be defined by our race, colour, gender or historical origins.'

'[This constitution] seeks to create the situation in which all our people shall be free from fear, including the fear of oppression of one national group by another, the fear of disempowerment of one social echelon by another, the fear of the use of state power to deny anybody their fundamental human rights and the fear of tyranny.'

'[This constitution] rejoices in the diversity of our people and creates the space for all of us voluntarily to define ourselves as one people.'[9]

These are very high hopes indeed. They will not be realised by words written on paper, not even if those words are the highest law of the land. They can only be realised by all of us citizens affirming our identity as

South Africans for black and white, Christian, Muslim and Jew, those of Indian and Malaysian origins. These particular cultural identities need to be placed by all of us in a broader, robust and vital sense of what it means to be South African. In both high moments of triumph and deep moments of despair we each of us know exactly the joy and pain of bearing this national identity. We need to make it work for us on all the days in between.

ACTIONS:

SUBJECTS OR CITIZENS?

Simon Schama gave his majestic history of the French Revolution a single word title: *Citizens.*[10] The revolution he describes is not just the story of a monarchy deposed and then executed; of a church stripped of its land and privileges; of an aristocracy denied both its title and indeed its station in society. It is also the story of a nation of French people being transformed from subjects to citizens. This is what the Tennis Court Oath meant, in which the members of the National Assembly swore an oath undertaking to remain in session until a constitution giving liberty had been firmly established.[11] The promise of liberty, equality and fraternity was made not just to rulers but to a nation of newly empowered and newly created citizens.

How many of the 48 million South Africans see themselves as citizens in this sense?

IDEAS:

MAKING THE NEW BETTER THAN THE OLD

How well did the new French nation of citizens do in their exercise of their new powers? Schama's epilogue in *Citizens* paints a dismal picture. The immediate aftermath of the Revolution was one of widespread violence of the most vicious kind; of deep economic decline; of a descent into general disorder. 'Was the world of the village in 1799 so very different from what it had been ten years before?' 'Had the Revolution at least created state institutions which resolved the problems which brought down the monarchy?' Schama asks. His answers are 'no' in each case. 'By contrast, the rural poor gained very little at all from the Revolution.' Indeed it took the military dictatorship of Napoleon Bonaparte to restore order, structure and progress to French society.[12]

How well are we South Africans doing after our negotiated revolution? In the Freedom Charter, the African National Congress equivalent of the French Revolution's Tennis Court Oath, the promise is made that 'the people shall govern'. Fourteen years after the end of apartheid, the progress from our divided and oppressive past is impressive. Apartheid society seems like a distant bad dream, designed and implemented by mad men from Mars. However, we are also far from the society that is the emphatic desire of nearly 50 million people: peaceful, prosperous and non-racial.

ACTIONS:
THE CITIZEN AND POLITICS

In the constitutional democracy that South Africa has become, the citizen is sovereign. In other words, the citizen is the ruler. The citizen rules through the political party representatives whom his or her regular vote sends to the national Parliament and provincial and municipal assemblies or councils. These bodies in turn elect the leaders of the executive institutions of government at all three levels. Both the legislative and executive institutions of government are held to account, as set out in our nation's constitution, by the courts.

Therefore the first duty of a citizen is to be an active supporter of the political party of his or her choice. This involves so much more than going to the voting station once every five years and casting a ballot. It involves joining or forming a political party which best represents the citizen's values and interests. It involves being an active member of that party, ensuring that both the policies developed and the leaders entrusted to advance these policies remain true to the original values and interests that commanded the citizen's support in the first place.

Without active members a political party becomes at best an empty shell, at worst a network of personal patronage. The authors' deep conviction is that the health of South African politics will critically depend on how well South African citizens discharge their duty to be political activists.

The democratic health of a political organisation becomes very evident when political choices have to be made. Both the ruling African National Congress and the Democratic Alliance have recently chosen new leaders in vigorously contested elections.

IDEAS:
ACTIVE CITIZENS BEYOND POLITICS

The role of the citizen involves more than his or her party political interests. As the African National Congress noted in its campaign theme in the national elections of 2004, the challenges we face are so huge, so fundamental, so all-embracing that they can only be achieved by a contract between people and government. Hence their key campaign slogan, 'A people's contract to create jobs and fight poverty'.[13] In our new democracy citizens have both rights and responsibilities. Rights are very ably set out and entrenched in our country's constitution in the Bill of Rights.

This Bill of Rights, which forms the second chapter of our constitution, guarantees rights in the areas of:
Equality
Human dignity
Life
Freedom and security of person
Freedom from slavery, servitude or forced labour

The right to privacy

Freedom of religion, belief and opinion,

Freedom of expression, assembly, demonstration, picket and petition

Freedom of association

Political rights

Citizenship

Freedom of movement and residence, of trade, occupation and profession.

It includes rights in regard to labour relations, environment, property, housing, healthcare, food, water and social security, children, education, language and culture; and finally the right of access to information, just administrative action, access to the courts, and rights in regard to arrest, detention and accusation.

A pretty impressive list!

The constitution is less clear on the citizen's responsibilities. In this, perhaps, our constitution repeats a mistake personified as it were in that single greatest icon of America, the Statue of Liberty. The distinguished American psychologist Viktor Frankl in 1970 observed that perhaps there was a need to build a Statue of Responsibility that would stand somewhere on America's West Coast, as a balance to Lady Liberty, who welcomes visitors and apprentice citizens to New York. (A citizens' foundation is hoping to erect such a statue somewhere on the US West Coast on 4 July 2010.)

The freedoms which democracy promises and the economic prosperity which citizens seek, are not established merely by words written in a constitution. South African society, as ordinary people experience it, does not seem like the kind of country set out in our constitution's Bill of Rights. The freedoms we seek from crime and poverty, as well as having access to quality education, healthcare and housing, require action from the people of our country. This involves both individual citizens and the institutions they collectively create. Rights, freedoms and laws must be given life in the lives of ordinary citizens. Sometimes this is in the individual life of a citizen as he chooses to offer or pay a bribe, or not; to obey the rule of the road, or not. Sometimes it is the citizen in the context of his or her family. Very often it is the citizen in and through social organisations she and he have created to promote their interests: trade unions, religious organisations, stokvels, residents' associations.

BEYOND THE TRIBE,
OUTSIDE THE GHETTO

DID APARTHEID END IN 1994?

Of course it did not. The political enfranchisement of black South Africans, and the adoption of a constitution that makes discrimination on the grounds of race and gender illegal, did not magically transform the life-experience of 48 million people. Neither of course were these events unimportant!

For those South Africans already alive in 1994, apartheid is a prison of the past from which it is not easy to escape. Even for those very young at the time, or indeed born after 1994, a pattern of race-structured experience persists. This is dramatically illustrated by the tragic events at the Reitz Hostel at the University of the Free State where students racially abused support staff. These events constitute a very extreme and perverse form of racism that remains widespread in our society.

It is commonly accepted nowadays that race is an empty concept in science. All mankind has a common history in Africa. At the level of DNA differences between races are superficial. New babies arrive in the world without race prejudice. However, race is one of the convenient contours along which greed, fear and prejudice can readily flow. This is all the more true when race coincides (as it often does in South Africa) with the economic characteristics of class. So black children who speak with a 'Model C' or suburban school accent become a race apart.

Where resources are scarce (and where are they not?) those with fewer resources will seek for the most obvious reason for their deprivation. So Christian Germans came to blame Jewish Germans for their economic and political woes in the 1930s even though German Jews were very emphatically German in culture, history, military service and other aspects. Black South Africans in Durban targeted Indian compatriots with racial anger in 1949 and again in 1959 even though Indian residents of Durban on average were actually poorer than the black residents of the city at the time.

There are many examples of communities mixed in terms of race, religion and class who have lived peacefully together for decades. These communities can descend into race, religious and class warfare in a very short time in moments of political and economic stress. The Indian subcontinent, both at the time of independence and partition, and today, provides good examples of this.

What then are the chances of realising the non-racial, non-sexist South Africa our very fine constitution describes?

IDEAS:

ON DIFFERENCE AND EQUALITY

Three hundred years of racially determined social reality will not be rebuilt in one or two short decades.

Patterns of human settlement are particularly enduring. One group occupies land over generations. The same is true of occupations.

The United States of America is the world's largest and most successful social melting pot. New York City, with the Statute of Liberty as welcoming icon, is the immigration capital of the world. Yet blocks of residential areas in all five boroughs of that city have a distinct race and cultural or ethnic character. And key economic occupations remain the homelands of particular race and nationality groups.

In a world that is often strange and threatening, people quite naturally seek the protection and familiarity of the known. Homeboy groups of race, tribe, religion and language provide some support, particularly when people move out of an 'original' community.

IDEAS:

GOOD CONTACT OR BAD?

Does contact between different race, religious and national groups increase or reduce conflict between these groups? History has examples of both increased and decreased conflict.

The critical issue here is the nature of that contact.

Where resources are in short supply (money, jobs, food and drink at a large event, etc.) the conflict for these resources – the battle between those who have and those who seek - will often become a conflict between groups wearing different badges of race, accent or religious dress.

A good example of this kind of conflict was the colour bar introduced in the earliest years of South Africa's industrialisation. This colour bar divided our country into race-defined contending camps. This division ran through all formations of our society. In the 1920s, in one of South Africa's most dramatic civil insurrections, the Communist Party combined with white Afrikaner nationalist workers under the slogan 'White Workers of South Africa Unite'.

The dilemma of building a non-racial future out of the construction materials of a racist past is equally present in the country's major opposition party. From its creation in 1959 the Progressive Party campaigned for a non-racial society which would involve the progressive enfranchisement of black South Africans, and through which black South Africans would be the major political gainers and white South Africans the major losers. With universal franchise now established, the Democratic Alliance finds itself cast as the defender of minority group interests in general and 'white' interests in particular.

These contradictions and tensions are an inevitable part of our unfolding history. How does the South

African citizen live out the values of our constitution in the midst of our racially defined and divided past?

Two guides seem useful: we need to be honest about our past, and creative and courageous about our future.

IDEAS:
SOME AMERICAN WISDOM?

Barack Obama, the first black American candidate for the office of President of the United States with a serious chance of success, made a remarkable speech about race relations in the United States. The speech deserves the close attention of South African citizens, for it tells us almost as much about race in our society as it does about race in America.

'Race is an issue that I believe this nation cannot afford to ignore right now ...

'the comments that have been made and the issues that have surfaced over the last few weeks reflect the complexities of race in this country that we've never really worked through – a part of our union that we have yet to perfect ... Understanding this reality requires a reminder of how we arrived at this point.

'As William Faulkner once wrote, "The past isn't dead and buried. In fact, it isn't even past." ...

'Segregated schools were, and are, inferior schools; we still haven't fixed them, fifty years after Brown v. Board of Education, and the inferior education they provided, then and now, helps explain the pervasive achievement gap between today's black and white students.

'Legalized discrimination – where blacks were prevented, often through violence, from owning property, or loans were not granted to African-American business owners, or black homeowners could not access FHA mortgages, or blacks were excluded from unions, or the police force, or fire departments – meant that black families could not amass any meaningful wealth to bequeath to future generations. That history helps explain the wealth and income gap between black and white, and the concentrated pockets of poverty that persist in so many of today's urban and rural communities.

'A lack of economic opportunity among black men, and the shame and frustration that came from not being able to provide for one's family, contributed to the erosion of black families – a problem that welfare policies for many years may have worsened. And the lack of basic services in so many urban black neighbourhoods – parks for kids to play in, police walking the beat, regular garbage pick-up and building code enforcement – all helped create a cycle of violence, blight and neglect that continue to haunt us.

'This is the reality in which Reverend Wright and other African-Americans of his generation grew up … For the men and women of Reverend Wright's generation, the memories of humiliation and doubt and fear have not gone away; nor has the anger and the bitterness of those years. That anger may not get expressed in public, in front of white co-workers or white friends. But it does find voice in the barbershop or around the kitchen table. At times, that anger is exploited by politicians, to gin up votes along racial lines, or to make up for a politician's own failings.

'And occasionally it finds voice in the church on Sunday morning, in the pulpit and in the pews. The fact that so many people are surprised to hear that anger in some of Reverend Wright's sermons simply reminds us of the old truism that the most segregated hour in American life occurs on Sunday morning. That anger is not always productive; indeed, all too often it distracts attention from solving real problems; it keeps us from squarely facing our own complicity in our condition, and prevents the African-American community from forging the alliances it needs to bring about real change. But the anger is real; it is powerful; and to simply wish it away, to condemn it without understanding its roots, only serves to widen the chasm of misunderstanding that exists between the races.

'In fact, a similar anger exists within segments of the white community. Most working- and middle-class white Americans don't feel that they have been particularly privileged by their race. Their experience is the immigrant experience – as far as they're concerned, no one's handed them anything, they've built it from scratch. They've worked hard all their lives, many times only to see their jobs shipped overseas or their pension dumped after a lifetime of labor. They are anxious about their futures, and feel their dreams slipping away; in an era of stagnant wages and global competition, opportunity comes to be seen as a zero sum game, in which your dreams come at my expense. So when they are told to bus their children to a school across town; when they hear that an African American is getting an advantage in landing a good job or a spot in a good college because of an injustice that they themselves never committed; when they're told that their fears about crime in urban neighbourhoods are somehow prejudiced, resentment builds over time.

'Like the anger within the black community, these resentments aren't always expressed in polite company. But they have helped shape the political landscape for at least a generation. Anger over welfare and affirmative action helped forge the Reagan Coalition. Politicians routinely exploited fears of crime for their own electoral ends. Talk show hosts and conservative commentators built entire careers unmasking bogus claims of racism while dismissing legitimate discussions of racial injustice and inequality as mere political correctness or reverse racism.

'Just as black anger often proved counterproductive, so have these white resentments distracted attention from the real culprits of the middle class squeeze – a corporate culture rife with inside dealing, questionable accounting practices, and short-term greed; a Washington dominated by lobbyists and special interests; economic policies that favor the few over the many. And yet, to wish away the resentments of white

Americans, to label them as misguided or even racist, without recognizing they are grounded in legitimate concerns – this too widens the racial divide, and blocks the path to understanding.

'This is where we are right now. It's a racial stalemate we've been stuck in for years. Contrary to the claims of some of my critics, black and white, I have never been so naïve as to believe that we can get beyond our racial divisions in a single election cycle, or with a single candidacy – particularly a candidacy as imperfect as my own.'

Perhaps the words most important for South Africans are those of William Faulkner: 'The past is not dead and buried. Hell, it's not even past.'

IDEAS:
XENOPHOBIA

May 2008 saw South Africa shaken by a wave of violence directed at foreigners. Starting in the township of Alexandra, this violence spread at the speed of a bush fire to all corners of Gauteng, and then around the country. According to police estimates the violence left 62 people dead, 670 people injured, and tens of thousands displaced from their homes.[1]

Has there been an uglier moment in the short history of our young democracy?

If we are to prevent the repetition of such violence in the future, we have some tough questions to ask ourselves. In reflecting on this sad set of events we need to avoid two unhelpful mindsets.

The first is the mindset that simply condemns the violence as incomprehensible, and a complete negation of our country's continental identity. This mindset calls in a high-minded way for South Africans to embrace their compatriots from elsewhere on the continent: to welcome them in.

In contrast there are the voices of anger which come from the areas where the violence took place. These voices told ANC President Jacob Zuma, when he was addressing a meeting on the subject of xenophobic violence, 'to leave and take his foreigners with him'.

The first voice – let us call it 'be nice to foreigners' – is the voice of our national elite. From their relatively safe suburbs and comfortable homes they tell people in townships and squatter settlements to share living and working space with newcomers.

The second – let us call it 'throw the foreigners out' - is the voice of those who argue that South Africa and South Africans must come first.

If we are to find a voice of sanity between these two extremes, a quite new pattern of interaction between new and old South Africans will be needed.

First, violent actions such as those seen around the country cannot be tolerated. We are a weakly policed society. At the very first indication of violence a rapid, massive and overwhelming police response was required. If the threat goes beyond what police resources can manage, the Army must support the police.

Second, if we are unable to control our borders, we should at least register foreigners crossing into South Africa.

The purpose of this registration is twofold. A temporary permission to enter the country should enable foreigners to remain in the country for a limited period of time (say two years as with the Commonwealth visas for young people entering Britain). It should enable these registered foreigners to seek work.

Third, we need to create a fast and simple route whereby foreigners can become South African citizens. Those that demonstrate a pattern of residence, economic activity and respect for our country's law should be able to become citizens. (After all, with the exception of the Khoi and the San, all South Africans were once *maKwerekwere*.)

Fourth, we must be quite clear that we expect foreigners to be employed legally, paid collective bargaining or statutory wages, pay their taxes and respect our laws, including those governing access to state benefits. We need to be as tough against employers, state officials and foreigners who collude to break or evade our laws, as we are accommodating to those foreigners who choose to play by the rules.

In doing all four of the things advocated above, we will be able to tell the present citizens of South Africa that law-abiding foreigners are contributing to economic growth, helping create jobs, and paying the taxes which provide services to South Africans.

IDEAS:
MOVING BEYOND OUR GHETTOS

All white South Africans have been shaped by our country's race history. Indeed, all white South Africans have benefited from the race bias in law, attitude, and access to economic assets and opportunity which was the very nature of apartheid society, whether they supported the two main parties that embraced racist laws or the small Progressive Party, the Liberal Party (forced to dissolve in 1968) and the banned South African Communist Party, all of which opposed them.

All black South Africans have been shaped by this racist past. This past will continue to shape black and white for generations. So the claim 'I am not a racist' is in fact dishonest and dangerous.

Equally we need to escape from a false equation that powerfully shaped past perceptions. Many nationalists, both white and black, argued that because people were equal they could not be different. Many liberals countered that because people were equal they could not be different. But elements of the equation need careful consideration.

Our nation is now built on the firm foundation of the fundamental equality of every citizen: black and white, male and female, both before the law and in the constitution: one single bundle of rights and responsibilities that apply to all. Our national Police

Commissioner, Mr Selebi, is equal before the law, as is the current President of the African National Congress, Mr Zuma. We have one set of laws and one constitution for all men and women.

However, that all citizens are equal does not mean that all citizens are the same. Each citizen is the product of the culture and context in which he or she was born, grew up and has lived out his or her South Africanness. In this sense we are one country but many 'tribes'. Language, religion, culture and custom constitute the architecture of our identities.

To deny the diversity of experience which is South Africa is as dishonest and as dangerous as negating the fundamental equality of rights and responsibilities of all. We must embrace both.

In very practical terms this means that most South Africans will tend to continue to live predominantly in 'own communities'. We are likely to live where our parents have lived; to speak the language of our mothers and fathers; to worship in the church, synagogue, mosque or temple where our parents worship. The majority of our friends (and perhaps work colleagues) will be people drawn from a similar background.

However, South Africa's many tribes have to share this one beautiful land with each other. If we are to be successful in sharing the challenges and opportunities of our country, we will need not only to live for much of the time in 'own communities', but also move out of these ghettos for at least some of our experience.

The ghetto: both prison and fortress

The world's first ghetto was established in Venice in 1516 as a place for the confinement of Jews. Venice's Jewish community was physically locked into this area each night from sunset to sunrise. This was merely the most obvious of a range of discriminations faced by Jewish people throughout Europe. Generally, Jews were unable to own land or practise a trade, and were limited to the professions of money-lenders (and subsequently bankers), doctors and lawyers.

Though Venice's Ghetto was most certainly a prison, it was also a fortress. Within the walls Jews were generally safe from violent attack, murder and rape, which were the fate of Jewish communities elsewhere on the European continent. The Ghetto was also for many preferable to the mass expulsion of Jewish people, as was their fate in England (in 1290 for 350 years) and Spain (in 1492 also for 350 years). Perhaps the case should be made for national apologies in these two nations for the shameful way they treated an important group of their citizens. Nevertheless the destruction of the Ghetto's gates ordered by Napoleon in 1797 was a liberation.

If we are unable to destroy the gates of our ghetto, can we at least walk through them as often as possible?

ACTIONS:

SEE SOUTH AFRICA THROUGH NEW EYES

In the first place we can make use of sources of information from outside the ghetto. South Africa is incredibly richly served by newspapers, radio stations and television, which reflect the experiences, views and interests of our country's different nations.

A citizen who regularly (say once a week) reads a newspaper from outside his ghetto will become more South African. Comparing the day's coverage in the *Sowetan*, *Business Day* and *Beeld* will give the reader a fuller and more balanced sense of what is going on in the world. It will also give him or her a sense of how different communities feel about different issues.

Listening to different radio stations, particularly to talk shows, enables the citizen to venture into other people's ghettos. This is true not only of those of race and language, but also the ghettos inhabited by different generations.

To watch a television newscast in a language other than your own is a good way of picking up some idea of another of our country's languages. It in fact 'teaches' language in exactly the way that small children first learn to understand language. It does this by associating a visual image with a spoken word. That much of the news coverage makes use of English makes this action even easier for those of little other-language skill.

ACTIONS:
DISCOVER SOUTH AFRICA OUTSIDE YOUR GHETTO

Our country is a patchwork quilt of different ghettos, and it is a quilt that is constantly changing. Most people are creatures of habit. They shop in the same shops, eat in the same restaurants, drink in the same pubs. A citizen who once a month visits a new country – a different shopping centre, a restaurant in a different part of town – will deepen his sense of his own country.

These 'voyages of discovery' should be governed by a real interest. For example, in Johannesburg some of the best Indian food is to be found in Fordsburg; some of the best jazz in Newtown; some of the best antique shops in Kensington.

ACTIONS:
MAKING FRIENDS OUTSIDE OF YOUR TRIBE

For most people who travel one of the richest experiences of the trip is getting to know people from the place visited, even if this is only the taxi driver or the tour guide. South Africans can have this experience without the expense or hassle of getting on an aircraft or paying for a hotel room.

Again, if contact between our 'tribes' is indeed to build a broad South African identity, then this contact should be driven by a strongly shared interest. Eating out with a work colleague at his or her favourite watering place will not only let you learn a little more about his or her ghetto: you will also have something to talk about!

The most satisfying experiences of cultural differences will be those that occur in the context of shared interests. The gym hour, the soccer team, a book club, all offer opportunities to understand both difference and commonality.

Increasingly, both working-class and middle-class suburbs are racially diverse. Working together to make these suburbs safe and pleasant will create a common agenda that builds bridges across ghettos.

An interesting area of cross-cultural experience is that to be encountered through religion. In the speech quoted earlier, Barack Obama reminds his audience that 'the most segregated hour in American life occurs on Sunday mornings'. Some 80 per cent of all South Africans see themselves as members of the Christian faith. This draws from every cultural, language and race ghetto. Do they worship together? Can they better share their diverse patterns of worship?

CONCLUSION:
DRAWING THE MAP FOR OUTSIDE THE GHETTO

As real as our ghettos are, so too is the country which they all share. The challenges of crime, the hope of education, the imperative of finding work and making money, the dangers of debt. Each of these is to be found in each ghetto. And none of these challenges can be defeated or achieved by the actions of a single ghetto. To defeat crime and achieve greater prosperity we need a coalition of ghettos.

Barack Obama described both the need and the hope of just such a coalition in the story with which he concluded the speech we have quoted extensively. We choose this story to end this chapter.

'There is a young, twenty-three-year-old white woman named Ashley Baia who organized for our campaigning in Florence, South Carolina ... one day she was at a roundtable discussion where everybody went around telling their story and why they were there.

'... Ashley said that when she was nine years old, her mother got cancer. And because she had to miss days of work, she was let go and lost her health care. They had to file for bankruptcy, and that's when Ashley decided she had to do something to help her mom.

'She knew that food was one of their most expensive costs, and so Ashley convinced her mother that what she really liked to eat more than anything else was mustard and relish sandwiches. Because that was the cheapest way to eat. She did this for a year until her Mom got better, and she told everyone at the roundtable that the reason she joined our campaign was so that she could help the millions of other children in the country who want and need to help their parents too.

'Now Ashley might have made a different choice.

Perhaps somebody told her along the way that the sources of her mother's problem were blacks who were on welfare and too lazy to work, or Hispanics who were coming into the country illegally. But she didn't. She sought out allies in the fight against injustice.

'Anyway, Ashley finishes her story and she goes around the room and asks everyone else why they're supporting the campaign. They all have different stories and reasons. Many bring up a specific issue. And finally they come to this elderly black man who's been sitting there quietly the entire time. And Ashley asks him why he's there. And he does not bring up a specific issue. He does not say health care or the economy. He does not say education or the war. He does not say he was there because of Barack Obama. He simply says to everyone in the room, "I am here because of Ashley."

'"I'm here because of Ashley." By itself, that single moment of recognition between that young white girl and that old black man is not enough. It is not enough to give health care to the sick, or jobs to the jobless, or education to our children.

'But it is where we start.'

South African citizens will discover the Ashley within if they are ready to spend some time outside their ghettos.

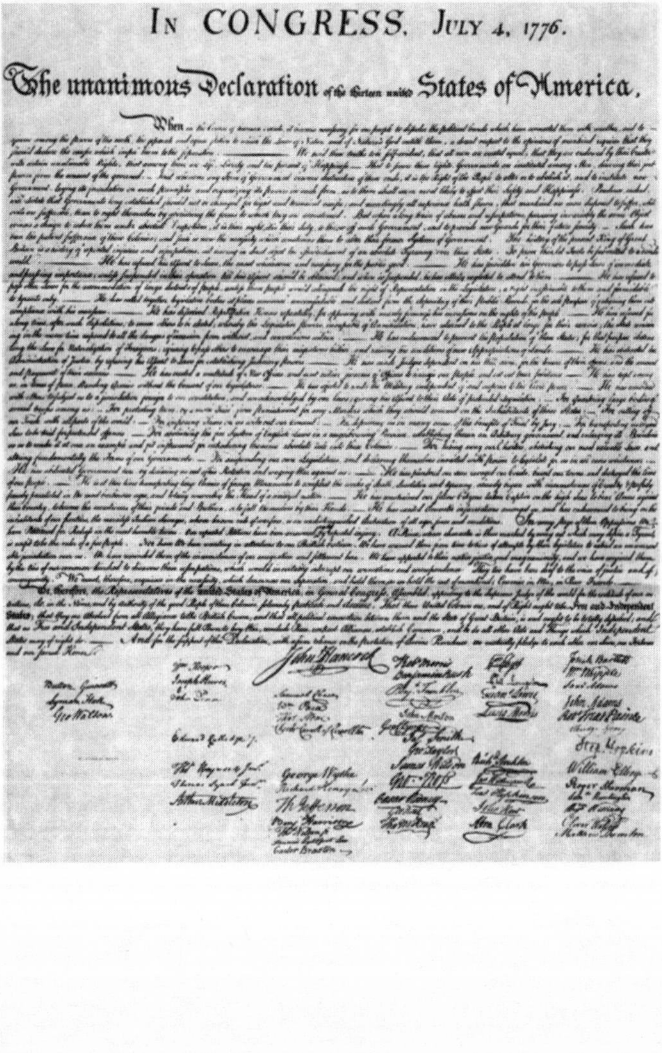

IN CONGRESS, JULY 4, 1776.

The unanimous Declaration of the thirteen united States of America,

CRIME

THE CHALLENGES WE FACE

Safety is mankind's first interest, need and priority. This has been recognized in every legal code from Hammurabi, the Babylonian ruler who is credited with one of the earliest forms of written law, dating from approximately 1760 BC,[1] onwards. When the people of the American colonies chose to declare their independence from the British Crown, they declared as their point of departure: 'We hold these truths to be self evident, that all men are created equal, that they are endowed by their Creator with certain unalienable Rights, that among these are Life, Liberty and the pursuit of Happiness.'

The South African constitution recognizes both the right to life and the right to freedom and security of the person, including the right to be free from all forms of violence from either public or private sources.[2]

IDEAS:
CRIME IS OUR URGENT PRIORITY

The first step in addressing any problem is to acknowledge that the problem exists. It is true that crime exists elsewhere. It hardly matters where South Africa ranks in the world crime league (though it clearly compares badly). The fact is that most South Africans live with both a reality and fear of crime that significantly undermines their *liberty* and clearly undermines their pursuit of *happiness*.

Our lived experience tells us the threat of crime is a real present danger for all South Africans all of the time. The most recently released crime statistics (April to September 2007) reveal that 325,733 citizens were victims of serious contact crimes, or crimes against persons. This involves the following crimes: murder, rape, attempted murder, assault with grievous bodily harm, common assault, indecent assault, robbery with aggravating circumstances, common robbery.[3] Citizens will draw limited encouragement from the fact that this is 5.1 per cent lower than the corresponding period one year earlier. Clearly, present levels of criminal activity are unacceptably high.

IDEAS:
CRIME IS A PROBLEM FOR ALL COMMUNITIES

Though individual crimes such as hijacking and murder

can be located in particular socio-economic locations (very different in these two cases), crime affects all. Criminals are no respecters of race or gender or class. The poorest areas of our country face the highest levels of violent and serious crime.

IDEAS:
THE CAUSES OF CRIME

The debate about the causes of crime is complex. Single-issue explanations are either wrong or unhelpful. If poverty was the only, or indeed the main, cause of crime, the poorest countries would have the highest crime rates. International crime rate comparisons are fraught with difficulty, and no robust set of statistics exists. However the statistics contained in a 1999 United Nations Survey on Crime Trends published in 1999 well illustrates the mismatch between prosperity and crime levels. Some of the world's poorest countries had amongst the lowest levels of reported crimes (expressed per 100,000 of population). For example:

India 179
Uganda 221
Lesotho 1,078
Zimbabwe 2,856.

In contrast much richer countries had much higher rates:

South Africa 5,106
USA 5,375

Norway 6,995
Ireland 6,276
Finland 7,273
Germany 8,025
Denmark 10,051
New Zealand 12,591.[4]

Even allowing for the significant issues of definition and efficiency of reporting, these rates of criminal activity suggest that crime and poverty are not directly or simply linked.

This is not to suggest that poverty is not a major moral, economic, social and political challenge for a democratic and progressive society. Reducing poverty is a compelling political objective in its own right.

A more compelling[5] link between levels of crime appears to exist in the demographic profile of a population. The United States experienced a sharp rise in its crime rates from the mid-1960s, followed by a marked decline from the mid-1990s. James Allan Fox, amongst many others, has argued the role of demography in both the increase and decline. The link is made to the most 'at risk' age grouping, i.e. males in the age group 14 to 25.[6]

Whilst both the logic and evidence for such a link are compelling, this explanation is hardly helpful in responding to crime. Given that young males make up a significant proportion of the criminal population, all programmes to keep them out of crime are clearly important. But neither the presence nor absence of such programmes is of much help to the citizen confronted by crime.

IDEAS:
BY THEIR TAX PAYMENTS SHALL YE KNOW THEM?

How much more easily would those living off illegal activities be exposed if citizens had access to taxpayers' data? The absolute confidentiality of tax information is set out in very emphatic terms in section 4 of Chapter One (Administration) of the South African Income Tax Act. A long tradition, and worldwide, has treated the tax affairs of citizens and companies as confidential. Why?

Perhaps a case can be made for the confidentiality of some aspects of taxpayers' affairs, for example the commercial data on which the calculation of taxation is based. But once the Revenue Service has arrived at the amount of tax due, and even more once this amount has been paid, what reason is there to keep this information from becoming public? In terms of the morality of taxation, citizens should be proud of the tax they pay. American colonists were moved to revolution by the slogan 'No taxation without representation'. Their absence of voice in the British Parliament which imposed taxes on both goods and services in the American colonies led them to refuse to pay these taxes. In a modern democracy is the reverse not equally true, 'No representation without taxation'?

Government makes use of tax data, for example in applying foreign exchange control. Why should citizens not have access?

ACTIONS:
GIVING THE CRIMINAL NO PLACE TO HIDE

Criminals live somewhere. Many take no effort to hide their lifestyle, and the benefits flowing from it, from their families, friends and neighbours. People know who the criminals are in their communities. By their silence they make crime possible. Citizens should not hesitate to report suspicions of a lifestyle supported by crime. Though Crime Stop promises protection for the source of its information, blowing the whistle on possible criminals does carry the risk of retribution, particularly where corruption has penetrated the police itself. We need to strengthen other avenues of reporting criminals, such as making use of religious organisations and other civil society bodies.

In arguing that criminals should find no hiding places in our communities, we need to ask: How effective are our communities? Let us consider this question with regard to four different areas of our society.

In the townships
Dense living, the challenges of poverty and unemployment, decades of political repression, and

Verdict for ZCC-bust killer

Alfred Moselakgomo

A Mpumalanga man who was bust by a Zion Christian Church (ZCC) priest when he went to the church for a cleansing ceremony after he raped and killed a teenage girl, was yesterday sentenced to life imprisonment by the Nelspruit high court.

Trevor Sazi Mashabane, 21, of KaNyamazane near Nelspruit, was found guilty of brutally killing his 15-year-old neighbour.

Mashabane apparently broke the padlock of the victim's door and repeatedly raped her while her mouth was stuffed with a pantyhose and her arms tied with tracksuit trousers.

"He then strangled her until she died," said police spokesman Captain Phillip Fakude.

Fakude said after committing the crime, Mashabane went to the local ZCC where he confessed to a priest and asked the church to perform a cleansing ceremony on him so that he could not be traced.

The priest pretended to go along with Mashabane's idea and asked him to return later, with a promise that he would arrange for priests from Moria to be present.

After Mashabane's departure, the priest reported the matter to the police, who arrested him when he returned to the church.

Mashabane was found guilty of burglary, rape and murder.

He was sentenced to five years for

LIFE SENTENCE: Trevor Sazi Mashabane

burglary, 20 for rape and life imprisonment for murder.

The ZCC welcomed the sentence, saying this was a clear message to criminals that the church would not cover up criminal acts. Church spokesman the Reverend Emmanuel Motolla said the incident also confirms Bishop Lekganyane's message that the church was not a sanctuary for criminals.

cultural traditions which place a high premium on good-neighbourliness have shaped the townships of our country into close-knit communities. Generally, people know their neighbours: who they are, where they work, where the kids go to school, etc. The street committees that came into existence during the 1980s (and at earlier times of our history) are a good example of this.

More recently, growing affluence, leading to many

moving from townships into suburbs, suburban schooling and in-migration of new groups including non-South Africans, may have undermined this knowledge. Nevertheless, it cannot be difficult for township folk to know what happens to their neighbours.

In the suburbs

Suburban life, in South Africa, and worldwide, is much more solitary. Generally few people living in the suburbs even know their immediate neighbours. Privacy is valued, contact minimal. This privacy has a price in regard to criminal activity. Efforts of suburbs people to get to know their neighbours and to understand patterns of movement and activity will pay rich dividends in terms of crime detection. Street committees would serve the suburbs well, especially if these were inclusive of those people who spend most time in suburban homes, domestic workers.

On farms

The incidence of violent crime in South Africa's farming community led to the appointment of a Committee of Inquiry into Farm Attacks in 2001. This Committee reported in 2003. The report notes that good statistics on the incidence of crime in rural areas, and violent crime in particular, are poor. Contrary to claims that farm attacks are racially motivated, the report suggests that robbery, particularly of money and firearms, was the major motive for such attacks. The report found that farm attacks were generally poorly planned and executed (compared, for example, to cash heists) and found no evidence for either the co-ordination of these attacks or a common strategy or shared plan. Finally the report found a very high degree of violence involved in such attacks, for which the Committee could offer no plausible explanation.

Cross-border crime, in particular stock theft

We use the term 'cross-border' here to describe both crime that crosses our country's national borders with its neighbouring states, and the domestic boundaries between privately owned farming land and communal rural land.

Some 28,742 cases of stock theft were reported in the 2005/2006 crime-reporting period (April 2005 to March 2006). In absolute numbers the highest number of cases (7,784) were reported in the Eastern Cape, followed by the Free State, with 4,435. However, if the incidence of stock theft is measured as a rate per 100,000 of population, then the Northern Cape reports the highest incidence (at 170) followed by the Free State (150) and the Eastern Cape (110).

Often this crime involves communities in organised reprisals, which in turn lead to violence. Reducing this crime is central to creating peaceable relations between neighbouring communities.

The absence of an effective and shared authority whose power runs on both sides of the border is a real barrier to the effective combating of these crimes.

The need to create real communities to prevent, detect and fight crime

All four kinds of society – suburbs, townships, rural areas and cross-border areas – share a common need: the need for close, inclusive communities that can combine to prevent, detect and combat crime. The spirit of the street committee needs to be revived in townships and created in the suburbs. People need to know their neighbours. They need to know their regular patterns of activity and movement. This will make the immediate detection of unusual activity possible. In the age of electronic networks we need a 'community' of street cell phone numbers.

The South African Police Service's website (www. saps.gov.za) offers information about farm attacks and rural safety. It describes the security structures that exist, including the old Defence Force Commando Units, and police Community Policing Forums. An honest appraisal must conclude that these 'systems' are hugely uneven in level of effectiveness and generally do not bring together the key communities who actually share South Africa's rural space, i.e. black and white rural communities. It will not be easy to bring together farm owners and farm workers, private farmers and communal farmers.

The price of not doing so will, however, be continued insecurity and high levels of very violent crime. What better common interest to create new patterns of community action than the shared desire to attack the scourge of crime?

Cross-border crime, particularly stock theft, poses particularly difficult challenges in the creation of anti-crime communities. The boundaries between South Africa and its neighbours, and between South Africa's nine provinces, are derived from geographic features. Some follow the lines of latitude and longitude, while others follow rivers or other features. Yet patterns of people's settlement have often been quite different, as are the patterns of human movement. Cross-border communities, with some authority to report and act on crime, will need to be created if the phenomenon of cross-border crime is to be effectively addressed.

In the area of tourism and game conservation our region now boasts a number of 'peace parks'. These are game conservation areas that stretch across national borders, managed by a single, shared authority. If we can do this to protect game, surely we can also do this to protect people and their property.

ACTIONS:
BOYCOTTING THE PRODUCTS OF CRIME

Economic gain lies behind most crime. Stolen goods need to be turned into money. Who buys these goods? The market for much of the most commonly stolen household goods, such as televisions, DVDs and other electrical appliances is well developed. The market for stolen cars is similarly well established. But citizens have a choice. If you buy stolen goods, you literally put blood on your hands. You become an investor in crime. And you should not be surprised if you become a supplier as well as a customer. Just say no to stolen goods. And why don't you report those who make the offer?

ACTIONS:
CRIME IN YOUR OWN NEIGHBOURHOOD

Knowledge empowers people to act smartly. This is very true in regard to crime. Individual citizens need to know about the nature of crime in their area.

National crime statistics are of very little use to individual citizens. The citizen needs to know about crime in his or her area. This is not difficult to do. Crime statistics are available for each of the country's 1,700 police districts. It is possible for the citizen to get information about the pattern of crime in the area where he or she lives or works. Crime is not evenly distributed across these 1,700 police districts. For example, of general aggravated robberies (robberies against victims outside their homes, workplaces or vehicles) 40 per cent are concentrated in just 5 per cent of the 1,700 precincts. In the case of carjacking, just 4 per cent of the precincts account for 40 per cent of hijacks. Murder, rape and assault have a different pattern.

There is much useful information to be gained about crime patterns beyond the precincts where crime happens. For example, docket analysis revealed that at least 70 per cent of carjacking occurs at the driveway gates of the home of the victim.

Knowing the crime statistics of your own area will enable you to get a factual handle on the extent of crime. Hard facts are a much better guide to both attitude and action than rumour, gossip and sentiment.

In this regard the police do need to do a better job in making crime statistics more readily (and speedily) available. A quarterly crime report by precinct made available in the month after the quarter end should be possible. In the authors' experience, heads of police precincts do share local data with Community Police Forums on a regular basis.

ACTIONS:
PARTNER OF THE CRIME BUSTERS

If it is useful to get to know the opposing team (the criminals), it is even more important to know your own team. This starts of course with the South African Police Service, and their most relevant 'face' is the police station where you live, or work, or both. There are many good reasons for visiting the police station, and no good reason to wait until you have to. Firstly there is the benefit of locating this important anti-crime resource. If you know where it is, it is going to be much easier to find it when you need it in an emergency. For example, if you believe you are being followed in your car, you can drive to the police station. Secondly, a visit to the police station will give you an idea of the resources available. What are the people, vehicle, and cellphone resources available to the station? What area does it cover? How many buildings, how many people?

If you are nervous about making the visit, go and enquire about the meeting times and venues of the precinct Community Police Forum (of which more later). Alternatively, visit on the occasion of one of your religion's high or holy days. There are most likely co-religionists working at the station and a modest gift of food, or even a greeting at Christmas or Easter, Eid or the start of Ramadan, Diwali, Yom Kippur or Rosh Hashanah, will be well appreciated. Our police men and women do dangerous work with great courage. They deserve our respect and support.

A third reason for making contact with your local police station would be to seek advice about crime prevention: security and alarm systems, avoiding carjacking, lighting. Again in the experience of the authors, the police respond both usefully and constructively to such enquiries.

Should your encounter with your local police station be a negative one, find constructive ways to bring this to the attention of police management. If phones are not promptly answered, calls for assistance not promptly responded to, if policemen and -women behave in ways that are either incompetent or discourteous, raise this with the station Superintendent in the first instance. And remember that as in any situation there are productive and destructive ways of complaining. Rudeness and anger seldom produce results. If you fail to get a constructive hearing, take this to the regional or provincial level. This is not only your right as a citizen. It is, more importantly, your duty. Be very clear what the unacceptable behaviour was, and be reasonable about the remedy you seek. In so doing you become part of a 'continuous improvement' process for the large and complex organisation that the South African Police Service is.

ACTIONS:
USING PRIVATE SECURITY RESPONSIBLY

Many South Africans hire the services of private security companies to supply an armed response, guarding or other security service. Like most things in life, private security companies include both the good and the bad. The well-managed and professional companies make an important contribution to the country's efforts to combat crime. The poorly managed, under-resourced and sometimes corrupt companies are worse than useless: they often are part of criminal networks.

A series of simple questions will help you determine the integrity of a private security company you intend using.

The first and most important question is whether

the company has vetted the staff for criminal records. One recent study suggested that a full 10 per cent of staff of a group of (the larger) security firms had themselves criminal records. Second, enquire about the skill base of the staff. Registered qualifications and training are required for each function. Two national bodies are available to check whether the company concerned is registered, and the individuals have the required 'certificates of training'. These are the Private Security Industry Regulatory Authority (www.psira. co.za), with which authority all businesses active in private security must register, and the Safety and Security Sectoral Education and Training Authority (SASSETA, www.sasseta.org.za), which quality-controls and registers all training for both government and private security providers.

Third, ask about the conditions of employment particularly of the people who will be providing you with services. If wages are very low, hours very long, and meals not provided, then expect the service to be poor, if not worse than poor.

As a visit to the police station will tell you much about leadership, resources, morale and preparedness of the police, so observing the dress, state of vehicles, communication skills and control room responses of the private security company will tell you a lot about how useful they are likely to be to you in an emergency.

ACTIONS:
JOINING THE CRIME BUSTERS

Citizens can join crime-busting teams. Here are three ways to do this.

Being active in a community organisation

South Africa is richly endowed with civil society or community-based organisations. In almost every strand of our history, local citizens have organised themselves in local organisations (the *small platoons* of civil society): religious bodies, youth groups, local branches of political parties, residents' associations, sporting bodies. These bodies are normally cohesive, united by a shared interest, command their own resources, and are capable of making decisions quickly. The governing bodies of schools provide a natural point of co-operation between citizens to ensure the effectiveness of the school, and in the context of this chapter the safety of teachers and learners both when at school and also in travelling to and from the school.

None of these small platoons were created with the purpose of fighting crime. Yet all have the potential to make a significant contribution to this end. These civil society bodies 'people' the area, often at interesting times of the day and night. They have local knowledge of the movement of people.

Community Police Forums

In recognition of local knowledge and local

resources, particularly human resources, the Police
Services Act makes provision for their role in crime
management. The structure which seeks to do this is
the Community Police Forum. Chapter 7 of the Act
sets out the objectives of this body:

'establishing and maintaining a partnership
between the community and the (Police) service;

promoting communication between the Service
and the community;

promoting co-operation between the Service
and the community in fulfilling the needs of the
community regarding policing;

improving the rendering of police services to the
community at national, provincial, area and local
levels;

improving transparency in the Service and
accountability of the Service to the community;
and

promoting joint problem identification
and problem-solving by the Service and the
community.'

Experience with Community Police Forums
(CPFs) has been mixed, and their establishment and
functioning are clearly uneven. At their best they are
clearly making an important contribution to crime
management.

CPFs exist at many but not all police stations.

Cutting the crime rate in Rosebank
By Sheree Russouw, 7 October 2008

DOROTHY Dorrangton has lived in Rosebank for 14 years, but she has never seen a policeman patrolling the region's streets. 'But the police must be doing a good job,' she says. 'There's been no trouble here for a long time. A lot of us "oldies" walk around here and we feel safe.'

In Rosebank, serious crimes have dropped by 66 percent, from 1,241 in 1999 to 854 this year. According to Eve Jammy, the chairperson of the Rosebank Community Police Forum (CPF), this dramatic reduction can be attributed to the workings of the forum, and the crime-fighting efforts of the 87 police officers stationed at the Rosebank Police Station.

Becoming a police reservist

It is possible to become a police reservist in four capacities:

- as a reserve police person, with uniform, firearm and appropriate training;
- as a support person, no uniform, no firearm and training where appropriate;
- in a specialised function such as pilots, doctors, divers, social workers or psychologists;
- as a sector policing person in a rural or urban sector policing programme, with uniform and training as appropriate.

To enrol as a reservist you need to be a citizen, a permanent resident, be between the ages of 18 and 70, be literate at least in English and have no visible tattoos! Reservists are expected to give 16 hours of service per month, complete appropriate training and attend station meetings once a month. You can apply to become a police reservist at your police station.

ACTIONS:
LIVING BOLDLY BUT WISELY

If we allow the fear of crime to become our constant companion, we will have constructed the worst kind of ghetto for ourselves. Our young nation is busy building itself. Our continent is like a teenage son or daughter: deciding how to dress, speak and live in his or her own way. We are living through an information revolution that is changing everything: how we live, how we work, how we gain and use information and knowledge. We live in a country of stunning beauty and rich physical diversity. All of this lies beyond the ghetto of fear. It would be a tragedy beyond words if we did not go out of the gates of this ghetto each day.

The only way to really live in South Africa is to live boldly. However, it is equally possible and very necessary also to live wisely.

For drivers, defensive driving skills are pretty much survival skills on our ever more congested roads. A range of commonsense behaviours can be similarly helpful in regard to crime. Draw money only at ATMs in the most secure locations (inside shops or shopping centres). Draw money at sensible times. Avoid driving in unfamiliar areas at night. Avoid carrying valuable documents, jewellery, etc., when these are not necessary to your journey. Regularly back up computer work (good advice in the age of Eskom anyway). Check whether you are being followed as you approach your destination at home or at work. If you think you are being followed, drive to your neighbourhood police station.

FINDING WORK:
MAKING MONEY

Our government has set itself two key goals for South Africa: to halve both poverty and unemployment by the year 2014. This chapter discusses just how these goals might be achieved, and in particular the role of the citizen in ensuring that he or she is economically active.

IDEAS:

IN SEARCH OF FIVE MILLION NEW JOBS

A research programme entitled Employment Scenarios, led by Human Sciences Research Director Miriam Altman, has been looking in detail at how employment can be increased and poverty reduced in our country. This programme, under way for a little over two years, has studied the sectors of the South African economy where additional jobs are most likely.

In October of last year the *Financial Mail*[1] devoted a special report to the work of the programme to date. To achieve the government's goal of cutting unemployment by half, some 5 million new jobs will have to be created. More new jobs will be needed to compensate for those sectors of the South African economy where employment is falling.

The *Financial Mail* journalist Claire Bisseker distilled the findings of the Employment Scenarios into eight key insights, briefly described below.

Insight One: Poverty will remain high

Even in the best-case scenario, with consistent 6 per cent growth rates through to 2014, and all the right policy moves, poverty will continue to be the economic fate of many South Africans. Currently nearly half of our population lives below the SA Treasury's suggested poverty level of R430 per person per month. Unemployment is not the only cause of poverty, as some 65 per cent of working people earn less than R2,500 per month. Social grants and an expanded public works programme will be needed to address the challenges of poverty even in a high-growth situation.

Insight Two: Public services need to expand

South Africa has a relatively small public service, and its growth has been modest in the first decade and a half of democracy. Given the extent of poverty, and the poor state of both physical and institutional infrastructure, a strong argument can be made for an expanded (but also much more efficient) public service.

Insight Three: New anti-poverty measures are needed

The scenarios canvass the possibility of a range of new measures including better basic service delivery (housing, water, healthcare, education) as well as the possibilities of government subsidies for basic goods (including basic foodstuffs), commuter transport and wage subsidies.

Already an impressive 12 million South Africans receive a social grant from government of one type or another, including state pensions.

Insight Four: Both the quality and the quantity of jobs matters

Low-skill wages have been stagnant or falling for most of the last 14 years. What is needed, particularly to address the country's anti-poverty programme, is more skilled and more productive jobs.

Insight five: The service sector is key

Many of our well-established industrial sectors such as agriculture, mining and manufacturing are declining sources of jobs. In contrast, service sectors such as tourism, hospitality and healthcare are growing. Indeed this research raised some important questions about how we think about the sectors of our economy. Cleaning services cut across industrial categories.

China has developed the construction industry into an export industry. We need to think carefully and creatively about the changing patterns of work.

Insight six: There is no silver bullet

The five million new jobs, after taking account of the sectors of the economy where jobs are likely to be lost, are not going to come from one law, one programme, one sector or one idea. The expansion of economic activity will take place, if it does indeed take place, over a wide range of activities. It will be organised in many different ways. Job providers will be many different sorts of people, organisations and institutions, both private and public.

Insight seven: Reduce the barriers to providing goods and services

People have energy and ideas. The more barriers that are placed between the providers of goods and services and those who want to buy them, the harder it will be for people to find work. The dramatic rise of hundreds of millions of people out of dire poverty in China well illustrates this, as is argued later in the chapter.

Insight eight: A cheaper/weaker rand may help but will not alone solve the jobs/poverty problem

Many developing countries have maintained a

relatively weak or cheap currency. This alone will not see our country ride out of poverty.

Three employment scenarios between now and 2014 are described. The first is based on an average growth rate of 3 per cent, the second 4.5 per cent and the third 6 per cent. Only the 6 per cent scenario (a tough ask in an energy-constrained South Africa) holds the prospect of reducing unemployment by half. For this to happen, growth also needs to take place in the most employment-dynamic sectors of the economy.

IDEAS:
LEARNING FROM CHINA

For the last four centuries South Africans have looked to the Northern hemisphere to find their compass in the world. The colonial empires wrote the script and South Africans duly spoke the words.

In these early years of the new millennium new parts of the world are moving to the foreground. The fate of the US and world economy is as much determined by where Japanese housewives choose to save as where Wall Street fund managers choose to invest. New economic giants are emerging in India and China. And in Russia a resurgent economic and political nationalism is evident.

For the moment almost all eyes are turned to China. Since 1978 China has adopted a strategy that puts rapid economic growth at the centre of everything. Following the social upheaval of the Cultural Revolution, China's 1.3 billion people have now embarked on a short march to modernity. No part of the world, including South Africa, will be untouched by this journey.

The scale of China's economic advance is both staggering and simply unprecedented. It constitutes 'a transformation that has lifted more than 400 million people above the poverty line of one US dollar a day since reforms began in 1978. Over the same period, the economy had recorded an average growth rate of 9.4 per cent, the highest of any large economy in the world. Whereas in 1978, private telephones were virtually unheard of, by 2005 some 350 million people had mobile phones and more than 100 million were accessing the Internet.'[2]

What can we learn from China's thirty years of growing prosperity?

First, the Chinese government has made massive investments in the country's physical and human resource infrastructure. By 2030 some 86,000 kilometres of national freeways will have been constructed (30,000 already complete), slightly longer than the US Interstate Highway system. The vast investment in physical infrastructure (roads, harbours, airports, energy, telecommunications) has been matched by an equally vast investment in human capital. 'Mainland (Chinese) universities produce more graduates each year than the US.'[3]

Second, at least as much of China's economic advance is the consequence of individual entrepreneurship as it is of government policy. A good example is Shen Wenrong, now the owner of one of China's largest steel producers. Shen in 2001 purchased (for $24 million) one of Germany's largest steel mills, disassembled it, shipped some 250,000 tonnes of plant 5,600 kilometres and re-assembled the plant in its new home in China. Shen comes from a peasant family, did not complete schooling, moved from his commune agricultural job to a job in a textile factory, and then with some co-workers set up (an illegal) small steel workshop.[4]

'Liu Yonghao, who by 2005 was the largest individual shareholder in the China Minsheng Bank ... was, back in the mid 1980s, using a bit of cash borrowed from relatives to start raising chickens on his balcony.'[5]

'Liu Chuanzhi, who ... bought the personal computer division of IBM in 2004, was (in 1985) just starting out as a sales agent for "Big Blue" (IBM) in China.'[6]

Often the individuals who have become China's super-entrepreneurs started in circumstances of great adversity: jobless, jailed, with the wrong class background. Generally, they were not *chosen* by the political elite to play this role. Indeed, more often than not, they operated outside existing policy, often illegally.

Third, this great economic leap forward has had many disadvantages. Chinese workers are very low paid, work very long hours, and are often exposed to unsafe and unhealthy working conditions. Much of China's economic growth has been based on the overproduction of very low-price, low-margin goods, often forcing Chinese producers to seek export markets to improve profit margins. Whereas China has been massively successful in penetrating consumer markets in America, Europe and Japan, much of the retail price goes to (non-Chinese) brand owners, marketers and distributors. China's economic growth has also come at a very high environmental price.

Of course South Africa cannot follow China (or any other country's path). We have embraced freedoms much bolder and more broadly based than has China. We have strong independent trade unions whose job it is to protect worker rights. We have strongly independent courts, media, etc. However, we cannot ignore an example so large, and so far, one that has had such a massive positive effect on hundreds of millions of Chinese people.

IDEAS:
NEW IDEAS ABOUT JOBS AND POVERTY

Ideas about finding work and making money are central for South African citizens. If we are going to create a better life for ourselves and our compatriots, we need government to make and effectively implement the right laws and policies; we need businesses that see employment creation as part of their value creation; we need trade unions determined to expand the number of South Africans who can find and keep decent jobs.

We need a national debate open to new ideas, but also a debate that learns the lessons of our experiences. Citizens will need to create and maintain the debate. They need to ask their political parties not just whether they support job creation, but how they intend to do it. They need to subject the answers to the critical review of track record and the citizen's own lived experience.

Our country abounds in plans, programmes and priorities. But planning is only the beginning of making progress. We need to be much more ruthless in measuring our actual achievement against the plan, and when this falls short, taking strong corrective action. If an agency fails to meet its targets over a period (say three years), let's scrap it and create something different. Why don't Cabinet Ministers set out their own objectives, and report regularly to the public against them? And a few, clear objectives would be more helpful than a 96 point plan!

Without a willing buyer for the good or service the job produces, the job cannot be maintained. The search for new jobs should therefore start with the search for new customers.

Equally, 'deregulation' is a slogan that needs debate, as does 'labour market rigidity'. If we want some jobs exempt from labour market regulation, we need to be ready to say what regulations can be exempted. Health and safety? Tax? Unemployment insurance? Unfair dismissal? This is not to say that regulation in all of these areas cannot be made both simpler to comply with and more effective.

There are other questions. Should South Africans be using technologies that replace people with machines as widely as we are doing? Why not return to parking exits manned by people? And ushers in cinemas?

Barack Obama is talking about 'patriotic employers' who do not export American jobs to foreign soil. We need to get companies to feel good about the jobs they create, and bad when they put people on the street. Cutting a workforce may lead to higher profits in the short term, but it carries the risk of social, political and economic instability in the longer term.

There will be times when companies need to cut their workforce to survive, where they have to adopt new technology in order to keep their customers. But in general we need an economic culture that sees employment as part of the broad process of wealth creation.

IDEAS:
FINDING/MAKING WORK

Individual citizens who want to find work and make money would be unwise to rely on experts, China or a deeper debate alone to achieve their goal. Individual citizens need to take their economic destiny into their own hands.

Even with the best policies, high growth in the right sectors, and the most favourable circumstances in global markets, many South Africans will be searching for ways to make money and create work. Others will be looking for ways of making money to supplement what they earn from their jobs. Hundreds of millions of people do this on every continent. In what follows we offer some thoughts as to how South Africans can think about making money and finding work. These thoughts draw extensively on a small booklet written by Ian Clark and Gillian Godsell when both were working at the Centre for Developing Business at Wits University.

Making money outside the context of formal employment involves selling a product or a service profitably. If this is what you want to do, you need to start by asking two kinds of questions.

THE ACTIONS:
GATHER YOUR RESOURCES

The first group of questions deals with opportunities and is about identifying the customer. The second group of questions revolves around the resources you have available. Clearly, these questions need to talk to each other. Resources without customers will make you no money. And customers that want things you cannot provide are equally useless.

Resources come in many forms, and even the poorest communities and individuals have some. You have some space – even if it is a balcony, or a patch of ground the size of a door. You have some skills. You have some time, which others may trade with you for activities they would rather not do.

ACTIONS:
EXPLORE YOUR OPPORTUNITIES

If your goal is to make money, then you are seeking to exchange your ideas, your resources (including your time and labour) for someone else's money. To do this you need to know what other people want and need badly enough to exchange their rands and cents for.

Information about what customers want and need is central to starting any business. Much can be gathered by simple acts of observation. In the shops in your area, which shops are doing well, and which are doing badly? What makes the difference? Inside the shops, which are the products that move quickly off the shelves, and which linger?

Often, how things are sold is as important as what is sold. Often real value can be created by finding new ways of meeting old needs. Again, observation can help the individual entrepreneur discover new products and new services with a new customer base.

As people in India moved out of rural villages and into the new and growing cities, someone in Mumbai (Bombay) realised that working men would no longer be able to enjoy the hot meal cooked by their wives, because they would be working far from their home. From this insight grew the Tiffin system of transporting the hot meal from the home to the place of work in time for lunch. In Mumbai some two million such meals are delivered each day using an informal system of couriers, known as tiffin wallahs, generally poorly educated and often illiterate, whose only resource is their time, and their ability to get around one of the world's most intimidating (and largest) cities.

Some years ago the Johannesburg municipality introduced new rubbish bins. These large plastic bins have wheels. They are easier to move than their predecessors, but they are difficult to clean. Some entrepreneur realised that this defect offered a business opportunity. With a small bakkie and some brooms he offers a service to clean these bins after they have been emptied.

Recently a new business offered a system for collecting videos and DVDs, contributing no doubt to the peace levels in many households. Dry-cleaning shops and depots have long offered a convenient place for people to drop off and collect clothes for cleaning on their way to and from work. The spread of the personal and home computer has created the opportunity for groups of computer-savvy young people to offer computer support services. Working wives have created a market not just for easy–to-prepare meals but for home cooking cooked by someone else.

ACTIONS:
DEVELOP ENERGISING NETWORKS

Networks are groups of people who share resources to achieve a common purpose. Networks can be useful in identifying opportunities to make money. They can also be used to mobilise the resources to respond to these opportunities. A school lift club is an example of combining and sharing resources to meet a common need. Networks bring people together who not only share a common purpose, but who also have a set of expectations of each other.

Networks can both create and destroy value. An energising network brings together people united by a common purpose, who also share a sense of reciprocal obligation. They are networks of people who each bring something to the collective feast. By contrast, dissipating networks involve a group of contributors (often the minority) and another group (often a much larger group) of those who consume. Families, including the extended family of brother, cousins and uncles, are good examples of both kinds of networks.

In an energising network it is vital that each member has a clear, and a shared, understanding of what the group expects from him or her; and equally what he or she can expect of others.

ACTIONS:
BE REALISTIC ABOUT YOUR CASH FLOW

When the entrepreneur has identified either a new need, or a need that can be met better, an important moment of truth occurs. There is a need for some arithmetic. Can you, the entrepreneur, provide the good or service at a price the customer will buy in a way in which you make, rather than lose, money?

Many businesses, both large and small, fail because of unrealistic costing. As a first step it is vital to work out the real cost of every step needed to get the product or service to the point of sale: the cost of materials; the cost of electricity and water, if these materials need converting; the cost of storage; the cost of packaging; the cost of your time, even if you contribute your time 'free' at the beginning of the business.

Once you are clear about costs, you need to think carefully about price. Here there are two critical considerations. As prices move from low to high, so customer demand will vary. Clearly, many products and services will have a price at which customers disappear altogether. Customers think about prices in at least two different ways. For the customer of limited means the money in her pocket is perhaps all the money he has for the whole month. This must be rationed around a range of needs. Her ability to pay will determine the prices she can meet. For the less constrained consumer a sense of value will be as important. What should I pay for a decent meal? How much should I pay for a

CD or a book or a movie or a pair of jeans or a pair of shoes? Except for the completely destitute and the richest tycoons, both factors – ability to pay and value – will play a role.

Customers can surprise in their judgements about pricing. Coffee drinking was revived in the United States when millions of people chose to pay up to six times the price of a simple cup of coffee for fancy coffees served in a new kind of coffee bar, Starbucks. Hundreds of millions of poor people in developing countries in Asia, Africa and Latin America have surprised economists by the share of their disposable income they have been prepared to spend on mobile phones.

All economic questions can be expressed in an equation that involves both value and volume. To make R1,000 in profit you can sell 100 gadgets at R10 or 10 gadgets at R100. It is important to note that the balance an entrepreneur strikes between value and volume determines not only price but also the cost structure.

MANAGING MONEY:
AVOIDING DEBT

The *Oxford English Dictionary* records the first usage of the word *economy* in the year 1530. The entry on *economy* notes the following: manager of a household, steward. Management of expenditure: originally of household.

The place where money matters most to the individual citizen is his or her household budget. The financial health or sickness of a national, regional or indeed world economy is, finally, the function of the health or sickness of the households it comprises.

Clever people (and professionals!) make money and enhance their status through making simple things complex. We often listen with undue deference to 'experts' pronouncing on important matters. Who has more authority than the economist?

Yet managing money is in fact very, very simple. The key principle was well expressed by Charles Dickens's fictional character (based on his father) Mr Micawber, in the novel *David Copperfield*. 'Annual income twenty pounds, annual expenditure nineteen pounds nineteen shillings and sixpence, result happiness. Annual income twenty pounds, annual expenditure twenty pounds ought and six, result misery.'[1]

Managing money (and other resources such as people, time, trust) is about striking a positive balance between what you earn and own on the one hand and what you spend and owe on the other.

Most people manage this balance well. However, there are aspects of modern society that have led many into the land of misery. Almost all of these have to do with reckless and foolish forms of debt.

A second area where good citizens are led into the land of financial doom is the sometimes hidden costs of ownership, or that great accounting truth that every asset is also a liability. In this chapter we shall examine what good citizenship means in regard to managing money.

IDEAS:

HOW MUCH DEBT?

> '*Neither a borrower nor a lender be,*
> *For loan oft loses both itself and friend,*
> *And borrowing dulls the edge of husbandry.*'
> – *Hamlet*

Polonius offers this advice to his son Laertes, who is about to set off for his gentleman's education in Paris. It is good advice. How much conflict and misery would be avoided if citizens could avoid borrowing and lending altogether? Sadly, how difficult would this be in our modern world, where an individual's credit record is the financial equivalent of his identity document or driver's licence. Yet if debt cannot be avoided altogether, at least it can be managed prudently.

What is the size and shape of South Africa's debt problem?

According to the National Credit Regulator, some 17 million South Africans have what has become known as consumer credit, but what is actually debt, which totalled 1.1 trillion rands as of the end of September 2007. (That is, 1,100 billion rands, or to put in all the noughts R1,100,000,000,000.00.) These are Zimbabwe-style numbers! On average each of the 17 million had three 'lines' of credit. By far the largest part of this was (home) mortgages.[2] Some 65 per cent of this debt is in the form of a mortgage bond (home-related); 13 per cent instalment sales (in old language, hire purchase); 11 per cent overdrafts and loans; and credit card debt at 5.5 per cent.[3] The size of this debt/credit 'economy' is growing rapidly, with mortgage debt rising 87 per cent, instalment sales 81 per cent, overdrafts and loans 36 per cent and credit cards an amazing 138 per cent over the 30-month period from January 2004 to September 2006.[4]

How healthy is this part of the national economy? In a press release somewhat optimistically entitled 'Majority of consumers in good standing with creditors', released on 27 February 2008, the National Credit Regulator revealed that of the 16.9 million 'credit active' consumers (i.e. consumers with debt) 62 per cent were in good standing. This group was made up of 7.9 million who were up to date with payments, and 2.7 million who had 'missed only one or two instalments'. The remaining 6.4 million South Africans had an impaired credit record (i.e. they were 'black-listed' with a credit bureau). Inevitably the burden of debt default falls heavily on the poorest section of the population. Nearly 54 per cent (more than half) of indebted consumers earning R3,500 have an 'impaired record'.[5]

The picture painted above of course represents the visible part of the iceberg. These are the people who have incurred debt with a registered credit provider. Millions more borrow money from informal and unregistered moneylenders, known as *Mashonisas*. No good statistics are available for this part of the iceberg, but everyday experience tells us that it constitutes a large part of total indebtedness.

It is important to note South Africa's 'debt economy' is not unique in its size. A common macro-economic measure of house debt is to express this as a ratio of household disposable income. In June 2006 this ratio for South Africa stood at 70 per cent. In contrast the United States, Britain and Australia all have ratios above 100 per cent. However, ratios such as these are of little comfort to individuals dangerously close to descending into a debt trap.

Debt is mainly a function of the actions of individual citizens. If we are to guide this behaviour, surely we need to discuss, debate and agree desirable *maximum* levels of debt. To do this meaningfully we will need to agree to some clear definitions of debt. No level of science will tell us definitively what the maximum level of debt should be. However, where science fails us, we can and should rely on common sense. Surely where household debt exceeds household income (the case in many rich and developed countries) we are in dangerous territory? And equally where households, individuals, businesses and governments spend more than they earn (i.e. are dissavers rather than savers) we are gambling with the future.

A group of wise women and men should suggest definitions and targets and a body like Nedlac should seek to reach agreement on desirable levels of debt.

IDEAS:

LIMITING DEBT: BEYOND INTEREST RATES

Governor Tito Mboweni has repeatedly warned South Africans against the growing mountain of debt they are busy building. The Governor has been particularly concerned by the impact that these very high levels of debt-driven consumption have on inflation. This 'debt mountain' is threatening to reverse the great achievement of the last 14 years: an end to double-digit inflation.

In a direct sense the only lever available to the Governor in terms of this rising debt mountain is to increase interest rates charged on debt. This the Reserve Bank does through raising the rate at which it lends to banks (the Repo rate).

There are at least two negatives associated with using only or even mainly interest rates to combat excessive debt.

First, it taxes (punishes) spending for consumption and investment equally. Borrowing money to start a new business should contribute to sustainable growth, create employment, and expand the tax base. Raising the cost of borrowing to fund productive economic activity slows growth and inhibits entrepreneurship.

Secondly, whilst high interest rates may (and eventually will) deter *new* credit extension, they also exact a very high price on existing debt. A positive aspect of higher interest rates is that they increase the value of saving, though the gap between rates of interest earned on savings and interest owed on debt remains a wide one.

The National Credit Act, introduced in 2007, provides an alternative model of curbing excessive indebtedness. For reasons that are not clear to the authors, the National Credit Act does not apply to credit card debt, probably the most expensive form of debt outside the Mashonisa system.

IDEAS:
DEALING WITH THE AMASHONISA

Though we do not know the size of the informal credit system known as Mashonisa, our experience of the real world tells us it is significant. We also know that this sector of our financial services economy charges outrageous levels of interest and employs vicious debt collection methods.

Here is a story that paints a vivid picture of the invisible part of the debt iceberg. It is taken from the Metal Workers trade union (NUMSA) website: www. numsa.org.za.

'At the end of 2004 two NUMSA members signed a loan agreement with a micro lender. In terms of the agreement, they would each be given two separate loans of R8,000 for building materials. In return they each had to pay R1470.72 every month for two years. They soon found that they could not repay the loan shark. By March 2005, the court had ruled that they pay back R35,963.15 to the micro lender.'

In terms of value each member agreed to pay R35,297.28 (R1,470.72 multiplied by 24 months) for R8,000 worth of building materials. If they had decided to use their own *time* instead of someone else's *money*, they could have saved the value at the monthly amount they had agreed on (R1,400) in just six months. Alternatively, they could have taken the two years they signed up for, and achieved their R8,000 of value over that period, saving just R300 a month.

Creating a responsible micro-credit industry out of the cloth of the Mashonisa will not be easy. But can our society afford to ignore this sector? There has been slow and painful progress with creating an economically viable and safer mini-bus taxi industry. Surely working with the institutions of civil society, particularly employers and unions as well as community-based organisations, we can make progress with the Mashonisa?

ACTIONS:

UNDERSTANDING THE TRUE COST OF DEBT

For many consumers the most widely used form of debt is that associated with the *credit card*. What is the true cost of using your credit card? The following example is based on information available on the Standard Bank entry level (blue online) credit card, for which a monthly income of R3,000 is required.

The example we use is the purchase of a set of furniture costing R2,000, making maximum use of the budget repayment facility on a credit card, i.e. repayment over 60 months. The current interest rate applied to this debt appears to be[6] 27 per cent per annum. This interest is calculated daily and is added to your account monthly.

By our calculations a purchase re-paid on budget terms on the entry-level card over 60 months would involve interest of R5,000 in addition to the principal amount of R2,000, giving a total cost of purchase of R7,000.

The second common way people use credit cards is as a *revolving form* of credit. That is, the repayment each month on a purchase is only a part of the total (negative) balance outstanding. Generally, credit card issuers require a very low minimum repayment, often 5 per cent and sometimes as low as 3.5 per cent. The result of making use of this part-repayment is that one stays indebted for a much longer period of time. For example, if a single debt were to be incurred and the minimum repayment made (at the 5 per cent level), the debt would take 20 months to repay. In fact the calculation is more complex than this, as interest is charged daily, and (at some stage) the principal debt reduces. If we use the 27 per cent interest on a major bank's entry-level card, a R1,000 debt would at least double in value, once the interest due had been added.

But it gets worse, for the habit of spending money you do not have is addictive, and so people normally 'fill up' the debt on their card as they repay. So the interest is perpetual.

It is important to know the true value of debt for two reasons. The first is the question of *value.* Is this television really worth R7,000 to me? Do you want to pay twice as much for the item you buy (twice the transaction value billed when you sign the slip) because you are paying over time?

In thinking about value, two realities are important. The first is to understand the power of compound interest. This is a matter of simple arithmetic. When inflation exceeded 10 per cent, the value of money generally halved every five years. Interest at anything above 10 per cent does the reverse to the value of your debt. And unless you repay at least all the interest due over the period between payments, your debt will grow, not reduce.

The second is to understand both the power and value of *time*. If you acquire or consume something with debt rather than cash, the value you will pay for this thing will be twice more than the cash price. Conversely, if you delay the acquisition and *save* so that you can pay the total price, or a significant part of it in cash, you will save on an equal scale. To paraphrase Charles Dickens, lay-by purchases result in happiness; purchases made on some form of hire purchase (which includes the use of a credit card with only partial and delayed payment) result in misery.

Credit cards are a very convenient way of using your money. They can work for you, but only if you very clearly understand their cost. Credit cards make most sense when you pay off the debt *immediately*, or when you receive your credit card bill. This can be as much as 30 days after you have made the purchase. Some cards offer longer periods of interest-free credit, some as much as 55 days.

Debit cards have all the convenience of credit cards, and neither the cost nor the debt trap dangers of revolving and budget style 'credit'. Debit cards enable you to spend the money in your savings or bank account. You can only spend what you already have. Would South Africa not be a better place, with a much sounder economy, and much happier households if the banks had introduced debit and not credit cards?

Let us take a second example to illustrate the (negative) value of debt.

Increasingly, new motorcars are advertised not at an outright price, but in terms of a monthly instalment price. Consumers need to understand that when they choose to pay in this way, they are exchanging money for time. They are using money they do not (now) have to acquire a car, whose cash price would be way beyond their resources. In so doing they will be paying much more than if they saved at the monthly instalment rate for a period. The period they would need to save (as with the Mashonisa) would be much less than the instalment plan, as they would not need to charge themselves interest.

Of course consumers have every right to make this choice if motor companies are prepared to sell their product in this way. They should do so with their eyes wide open. Perhaps a way to illustrate this point would be to realise that if you pay for the car before acquiring it, you could buy twice the car you buy on instalment.

ACTIONS:
HOW MUCH DEBT CAN I AFFORD?

The National Credit Act became fully effective in

our country in July 2007. One of the critical concepts introduced by the law is the concept of *reckless credit*.

Section 80 of the Act (No. 34 of 2005) defines reckless credit, inter alia, as:

'(b) (i) the consumer did not generally understand or appreciate the consumer's risks, cost or obligations under the proposed credit agreement; or (ii) entering into that credit agreement would make the consumer over-indebted.'

Section 81 requires the credit provider to assess the issue of over-indebtedness. Other sections of the Act require the credit provider to disclose the total costs of debt fully.

The great advance of the National Credit Act is that it brings the legal responsibility for reckless credit in line with moral responsibility. That is, a legal culpability resides both with the credit provider and with the consumer. If a credit assessment has not been completed, or if it has been and it shows that the credit will leave the consumer over-indebted, then the agreement entered into becomes essentially unenforceable.

The National Credit Act also creates new and much better mechanisms to deal with consumers who become over-indebted, with a Tribunal and Debt Counsellors able to assist consumers in re-scheduling their debt.

However, these provide new ways to resolve debt problems only once they have occurred. The responsible citizen will want to avoid getting into over-indebtedness in the first place. So the key question becomes: how much debt can I afford?

We all know that we need money to live. The money we use to live can come from two sources. The first is the money we earn: through a job, a pension, a state grant, a business activity, and some investments. The second is the money we borrow. Borrowed money comes with two kinds of risk. Firstly, at some stage we have to repay the loan: give back the money to the person who has provided it. Secondly, while we are using this money, and before we have repaid it in full, there is a charge for borrowed money that is called interest.

It is useful to look at how businesses think about these two sources of funding business activity. The money that belongs to the owners of the business is called 'owner's equity' or 'own funds', and is reflected on the company's balance sheet as an asset. Money borrowed from banks, customers, suppliers or other sources, which is required to be repaid at some stage, is described as borrowings, and is reflected as a liability on the company's balance sheet. The ratio of own funds to borrowed funds is used to describe a company's gearing. This gearing is really an indication of the company's financial risk profile. If own funds are 100 and borrowings are 50, the company would have a gearing of 50 per cent. Different kinds, sizes and stages of business can afford differing risk profiles. However, gearing beyond the 30–40 per cent level would be generally regarded as high risk.

In regard to the second risk of borrowed money, the interest you have to pay while using this money, a second measure is commonly applied in business. This is normally referred to as interest cover, and seeks to measure the ability of the business to pay the interest charges due on its borrowings, from the income it generates.

The citizen's balance sheet and income statement

Individual consumers would benefit from drawing up a simple balance sheet: a statement of what they own and what they owe at a moment in time. This balance sheet would allow them to understand their personal debt gearing, and from this their risk profile. For most of us, a gearing beyond the 30 per cent level would suggest a high degree of risk. In the second simple exercise the citizen consumer writes down everything he or she earns in a period (a month and a year are two useful periods) and everything she or he spends. This enables the consumer to calculate his interest cover. Both measures are important, but the interest cover is critical. If confidently expected income does not exceed interest repayments (and in this case principal debt and interest repayments, such as the credit card budget and minimum repayment), then the consumer is headed for default, black-listing and ultimately insolvency and sequestration.

When people look at investing in a business they would expect income to exceed interest charges by a significant multiple, e.g. four, five, six or seven times, depending on the business's profile of other risks.

Consumers should set themselves the goal of having monthly real disposable income at least several times that of their monthly debt repayments.

We need now to pause on the concept of *disposable income*. In deciding how much debt you can afford, this means income not already pledged to another use: income after rent, food, petrol, school fees, entertainment, etc. Clearly, the most emphatic source of disposable income is money that is saved and not spent. Accumulated savings are immediately available. Regular savings (particularly after these have been achieved over a period) are the second most secure source of disposable income. The simple hope that we will spend less than we earn is the most dangerous source!

In order to decide how much debt you can afford, you need to do the two exercises suggested above. In creating a personal balance sheet, simply write down everything you *own* and everything you *owe*. This will tell you how much room you have for further borrowing. In creating a personal income statement, write down everything you earn in the average month and over the forthcoming year, and then write down what you intend to spend in each of these two periods. This will tell you how much debt you can service.

In each case you would be wise to provide for the unexpected: health problems, marriages, funerals, and teenage expense accounts!

ACTIONS:

THE MOTHER OF ALL DEBTS:

HOW MUCH HOUSE CAN YOU AFFORD?

Generally, interest charged on debt changes over time, linked to what the banks and borrowers themselves have to pay for money. As a house mortgage bond is by far the largest debt for the individual, changes in mortgage interest rates very substantially change mortgage repayments. As South Africa finds itself in a period of high and rising interest rates, home purchasers should provide for an increase (perhaps substantial) in mortgage interest rates.

In fact the South African Reserve Bank's repurchase rates (the Repo rate) have risen by 400 basis points, or from 7 to 11 per cent from July 2006 to December 2007, an 18-month period. This is rate at which the Reserve Bank lends money to commercial banks. These banks (the primary source of home mortgages) generally follow rate movements made by the Reserve Bank, though predictably their 'base rate' for mortgages is higher than the Reserve Bank Repo rate. Over this same 18-month period prime overdraft rates moved from 11 to 14.5 per cent. Two examples illustrate this point.

A thirty-year bond of R1,000,000 at an 11 per cent interest rate requires a monthly repayment of R9,523. At 3.5 points higher interest, i.e. 14.5 per cent, this monthly repayment rises to R12,245, or by R2,722 or 28 per cent higher.

A bond of similar period (thirty years) for R500,000 requires a monthly repayment of R4,761 at 11 per cent interest. At 14.5 per cent interest this rises to R6,122, or by R1361, again 28 per cent higher.

The world is an uncertain place. Many factors cause Central Banks to raise their interest rates. Citizens who take out a mortgage loan to buy a house would be wise to anticipate an increase in their monthly repayments of up to 30 per cent.

HOW LARGE A HOME LOAN CAN I AFFORD?

The ratio applied by the banks is that repayments cannot be more than 30 per cent of disposable income. However, the more meaningful test for the citizen consumer is the amount of *free cash* he or she has to pay off the bond each month. Here free cash means cash not already allocated to another spending purpose. One of the bank's loan application forms provides a list of 'other expenditure'. It is an intimidating list:

PAYE
Pension deduction
UIF deduction
Medical Aid deduction
Insurance premiums (household, vehicle, homeowners, cell phone, funeral, medical)
Life assurance premiums
Electricity and water, rates, taxes and levies,
Accommodation rental

Hire purchase agreements
Telephone and cell phone
Alimony or maintenance
Donations
Pocket money
Education
Clothing
Groceries
Medical bills
Domestic service wages
Security
Transport
Entertainment
TV rental
Retail store accounts.

Free cash is what is left after all the above needs have been met. And this is the amount of additional debt the citizen consumer can afford to take on, including new debt on a home loan.

ACTIONS:
PLANNING FOR THE MAINTENANCE OF YOUR ASSETS

In accounting terms every asset is also a liability, or has a matching liability attached to it. This is what is meant by double-entry bookkeeping. In life this is equally true. This side of heaven, all things have a strong tendency to deteriorate, decay and indeed to descend into chaos. In physics this is captured in the law of entropy.

All first-time homeowners experience this truth most vigorously. When the house payment is made (or the bond secured), lawyer's fees discharged and insurance secured, the first-time homeowner breathes a huge financial sigh of relief. And then ... the gutters need replacing, the geyser fails, a toilet blocks, and so on.

Two concepts are important here. Firstly, every asset (and thing) in life has a limited (useful) life. Again an accounting concept is helpful: depreciation requires the owner to determine the 'useful life' of the asset and reduce its value over that period. If the asset is essential to the conduct of a business (or the living of a life), then the owner must also provide for its replacement at the end of that life.

There is no need for the citizen to do this for every asset they own: only those reasonably large items essential to their and their family's lifestyle. Clearly this would be true of a motor vehicle. The useful life will depend on both the owner's 'taste' and his or her competency as an owner. If it is the owner's desire to drive an up-to-date vehicle, he or she might decide the life of a newly purchased vehicle is as little as three years. If he or she is not equipped to ensure the maintenance of the vehicle through its ownership life, then a life of more than five years is unlikely. Unreliability and repair costs make purchasing a new vehicle attractive. Those owners of strong mechanical ability, in contrast, might well keep a vehicle for ten years or more.

The citizen will know the kind of owner he or she is. A life can be determined.

Vehicle maintenance has a cash-flow effect as well. Unless a maintenance plan is purchased, some money needs to be set aside for regular servicing and incidental repairs. Even with the maintenance plan there will be costs of owning a vehicle not covered, such as the replacement of tyres.

And what about replacing vehicles? Those who allocate a relatively short life to their vehicles (three to five years) will want to take note of the re-sale or trade-in value of their car. Tables of these values are available from the manufacturers and from the AA.

Regrettably the price of cars (certainly new cars) tends to rise rather than fall. The owner should provide at least for the inflation effect of the time period to replacement, unless he or she is prepared to 'buy down'.

In regard to houses there are a limited number of regular maintenance issues such as painting, roof repair, cleaning and fixing gutters. There may be other 'one off' issues such as damp proofing or re-wiring. Those who plan for at least some of the surprises houses present will cope better than those who do not.

Probably a third area in which both maintenance and replacement are important concerns computers and telecommunications, especially if these are an important part of the citizen's business and social life.

Here the good news is that electronic goods are one area in which unit prices have been reducing over time. Often, however, this cost reduction is outweighed by new technology. Particularly with regard to mobile phones, citizens would be well advised to understand the total cost of ownership, in terms of the cost of the mobile phone itself, monthly rental and service fees, and per-call costs.

EDUCATION

It is a deep-seated and universal desire to want to give your kids the best start in life. And clearly the 'gift' of a good education is a critical part of that good start. It is a gift once given that can never be taken away. It is never used up.

IDEAS:

WHAT MAKES FOR A GOOD EDUCATION

What does a good education mean? In part it is the piece of paper (school-leaving certificate, university degree) that gives entry to better opportunities and status in society. In part it is an inherent set of abilities that enable a person to design his or her own destiny.

This set of inherent abilities consists of at least three bundles of competencies. The first is a specific set of skills: the ability to read and write; the ability to take a university entrance exam; the ability to undertake a set of technical tasks such as those mastered by artisans such as electricians, plumbers, etc. The second is a more general set of thinking capacities, often described as problem-solving skills: knowing where to acquire the knowledge we at the moment do not have; the ability to figure out the solution to a problem whose answer is not already known. The third is a set of values about how to conduct oneself in a society.

A good education involves skills, competencies and values. The school, college or university alone cannot provide this.

IDEAS:
SCHOOLING OUTSIDE OF SCHOOL

Ivan Illich published his essay *Deschooling Society* in 1971. It is a critique of the negative consequences of mass, compulsory schooling that in 2008 continues to make powerful arguments, and should make educators aware of the damage and shortcomings of mass education systems. For our purposes Illich makes the important point that much learning happens outside the context of school.

'Most learning happens casually, and even most intentional learning is not the result of programmed instruction. Normal children learn their first language casually, although faster if their parents pay attention to them. Most people who learn a second language well do so as a result of odd circumstances and not sequential teaching. They go to live with their grandparents, they travel, or they fall in love with a foreigner. Fluency in reading is also more often than not a result of such extra-curricular activities. Most people who read widely, and with pleasure, merely believe they learned to do so in school; when challenged, they easily discard this illusion.'[1]

Illich argues that most learning occurs in the context of leisure and work, rather than in the process of formal 'learning' in an educational institution such as a school. For children this context is, importantly, the context of family and home.

Most parents will not take Illich's advice to take their children out of school. They will benefit from his wisdom, though, in focussing on the critical educational role of the home.

What then is a good learning home? In traditional agrarian societies the homestead provided clearly defined roles for children. These roles involved both work and play. They involved a significant interaction with the adults in the homestead in a way that demonstrated skills, competencies and values.

In urban, industrial society many of these roles have disappeared. Children may be incorporated into the work programme of the house, though not always in ways that teach skill, competency or values. And the pattern of interaction between parent and child is often minimal. Remember Illich's words about the learning of the first language. This occurs faster, he says, 'if their parents pay attention to them'. Indeed, the parent is the first (and probably most important) educator. Does he or she engage the child in a conversation? In discussion, are judgements, opinions, prejudices and conclusions called into question? Does the parent draw the child into the world of information and ideas; discuss a newspaper article, a radio programme, a television debate, or what is happening in the street, township, suburb or community? In the digital world in which we live, does the child have critical access to the world of computers and the Internet? No source of information or ideas is inherently good or bad. Each source of information can be used well or badly.

Skill can be taught by drill. Stripping a clutch is best taught by doing. Competence and value can only be 'taught' (if taught at all) through a process of continuing engagement. Does the parent encourage reading, and know what is read; encourage listening or watching the electronic media and know what is heard and seen? It is in debate and discussion that true learning takes place. At its best this will always be both an individual process and a spontaneous one. It is so much more likely to occur in the context of the home than in the context of the classroom.

Parents inhabit the world of work and society. Teachers exist in the world of the school. Parents do, know and experience things which teachers cannot. If parents do not make this experience available to their kids, their kids will have a much less rich and real understanding of the world for which they are being educated.

If a child does not have a rich learning experience outside school (home, community, relatives, work), her or his education will be partial, stunted and incomplete. Education at school needs both a foundation and context of learning outside of school, and most particularly in the home.

IDEAS:

WHAT MAKES FOR A GOOD SCHOOL?

Notwithstanding Ivan Illich's desire to 'deschool' society, most parents will want to see their children learning in good schools, as well as learning at home, at work and at play. South Africa offers parents considerable choice in finding the right school for their children. The country's schooling system has some 12 million learners, nearly 400,000 educators in nearly 27,000 schools. Some 26,000 are state or public schools, 1,000 are private. The range of choices is in fact daunting.

Public or Private

In regard to private schools there is no constraint of geography or 'zoning'. Those schools with boarding establishments offer complete geographic (indeed continental) freedom, though at considerable expense.

Broadly, private schools divide into two groups: the older, expensive and well-resourced and the newer, and less expensive (sometimes inexpensive) with very variable resources. The more established schools generally belong to the Independent Schools of South Africa Association (ISASA). The ISASA website (www. isasa.org) offers considerable information about this group. In general the schools belonging to this group are very well resourced, have small class sizes and well-qualified teaching staffs. With few exceptions, they are also expensive. Though generalisations are difficult annual fees are unlikely to be less than R50,000 per annum, and R100,000 for boarding.

The second group of private schools have mainly been established in the last decade, have a student population which is predominantly black, and charge fees of less than R20,000 per annum, many much less.

The 26,000 state or public schools can be divided into three broad geographic categories: suburban schools, township schools and rural schools. They are generally much larger than the established private schools and much less well resourced, though in each of these three categories a wide divergence in quality is to be found. Whilst some elements of geographic 'zoning' may constrain choice, most schools work hard to accommodate parent choice.

IDEAS:

RURAL SCHOOLING AND EDUCATION

Poverty is most concentrated in South Africa's rural areas. These areas have the highest rates of unemployment. Urban migration means that the very old and the very young remain in these areas, and often the only economic activity is highly unproductive subsistence agriculture.

It should therefore be no surprise that education in rural areas faces particular challenges. These challenges demand responses from those South Africans who have achieved success and risen to prominence, for whom a particular rural area remains home, even though they no longer live there. Those key individuals who may now be in business or in government or even in the private sector need to mobilise to make a difference to the rural towns and villages which are their origins.

There is no doubt that rural development has the potential to be a very feasible way of slowing down migration to the cities. Through this kind of development, rural populations may have the possibility of prospering, therefore cutting down on migration. There is no better way of improving rural areas than focusing our efforts on improving rural schooling and education.

The lack of education for many in rural areas translates into economic poverty. Without education, there is no hope for rural children to break the cycle of poverty.

Education not only produces social change, but it also facilitates development. It is only through education that students' creative participation and critical thinking are developed, and this will equip them to face the future.

The challenge for our rural champions is to ensure

that in their hometowns and villages there are functional schools, accessible to all.

Rural schools face a range of challenges. Key teaching facilities such as computer laboratories, libraries, sports facilities as well as proper lighting are often lacking. Rural schools often lack funds and fundraising skills. Their buildings are in a state of decay. Limited schooling takes place because children come to class sporadically. Teachers may go to class drunk and behave abusively towards learners.

Principals are often weak and ineffective. Members of school governing bodies, especially parents, sometimes do not understand their role in these structures.

The problems of rural education can only be tackled community by community. Many successful South Africans have a strong anchor in a rural town or village. If each 'homeboy' or 'homegirl' was to take a sustained interest in the schools now operating in this town or village, they could:

• Ensure that the school has a dedicated and professional head teacher, who has been exposed to leadership training, has some basic understanding of finance, and is accepted into the community as an important community leader. Without effective leadership the school will not function well. Part of ensuring this leadership is enabling the school head to live at or close to the school. The community can provide land and housing to this end.

• Ensure that the school has a governing body that understands its responsibilities and has the training and skills to exercise the considerable powers of a school governing body effectively.

• Ensure that the school has a group of professional and dedicated teachers. In this regard both community respect and the opportunity to live in decent accommodation close to the school are important.

• Ensure that the physical facilities of the school grow in quantity and quality each year, and that these facilities are maintained.

• Ensure that learners, educators and parents all understand their roles, and commit to a code of conduct to exercise their responsibilities effectively.

This is a formidable agenda, but it is by no means impossible. Those rural benefactors who are employed in either government or the private sector have regular access to leadership training resources. For a company to send some of its training staff to train head and other teachers in a rural school would bring benefits to both parties. Both government and NGOs have access to relevant training materials in regard to the role of governing bodies. The work of improving and maintaining buildings could be organised around visits home.

Many private sector companies now promote volunteerism amongst their employees. Under these schemes employees volunteer for charitable work with the company, contributing money or time. Why shouldn't rural schools be part of such schemes?

The challenge to the rural community

Three critical issues can only be tackled by the rural community themselves.

The first is to make the school an economic asset, at least for the school itself. In rural areas learners often have a long journey to school, without time or opportunity for a morning meal before setting out. Rural schools normally have access to agricultural land and agricultural activity. Chicken fattening, where an organisation acquires day-old chicks and looks after them until they are fully grown, is but one example of possible agricultural activity. These economic activities can draw on both the labour and knowledge of local (otherwise economically inactive) employees. Such activities could well develop into a school-feeding programme, which should make use of local labour and local resources. In principle such programmes should qualify for government funding, though the programme should be possible without external funding.

The second is to ensure that the community feels ownership of the school, and that the school is valued by the community. The head teacher should be a valued leader in the community, assisting the community in its relationship with government at local, provincial and national level. Teachers should be a resource, perhaps participating in adult literacy programmes, and in this way supplementing their incomes. The school facilities, hall and computer facilities could be a community resource with the possibility of earning the school some income.

Thirdly, the community must ensure that no child stays out of school. This may have financial implications. Where schools need to charge school fees, the broader community (including those from the area now moved on to their urban lives) should be able to assist those who are unable to pay fees. The community is the ultimate effective lobby in ensuring that government funds schools adequately.

Each of these three challenges requires leadership, and those now living outside the community and having access to knowledge and experience and other resources will be in the best position to provide leadership.

IDEAS:
QUALITY VERSUS ACCESS

Much of the debate about post-apartheid education has been focused around two very important but complex ideas.

Some commentators have focused on the quality of education being offered. Others have looked for policy measures that will ensure universal access.

We need to examine both these concepts critically if we are to define the education road we want to move along.

If a good or quality education deals in the currency of skills, thinking capacity and values, it is these three things we should look for and these three things we should seek to measure when discussing quality.

A study by the international consulting group McKinsey in 2007 came to the unsurprising conclusion that the single most important criterion for educational quality was the quality of teachers. The everyday experience of most people would confirm this. McKinsey also concluded that critical to teacher quality was attracting people who really wanted to teach – in other words, teachers with a vocation. Vocations are both socially endorsed and individually chosen. Pay is a measure of social endorsement. An adequate level of pay is needed for dedicated teachers to stay in teaching. A teacher should be able to support his or her household as main breadwinner. Pay alone will not establish the social worth of this profession.

It is a cliché that teachers shape the fate of nations. But remember, a cliché is an oft-repeated truth. There are many ways in which the teacher's role in society can be affirmed (or undermined). Social status is also closely linked to class. In rural communities and amongst the urban poor and working class, teaching continues to occupy a respected place in society. In middle- and upper-class communities different career choices tend to dominate.

In regard to developing thinking capacity diversity and difference have a vital role to play. If the class is completely homogeneous, much of the social reality of the class is likely to go unchallenged. Difference creates dissonance and requires reflection and thought.

In terms of values, where the classroom is composed in very different race, class and religious terms from the society as a whole, it is unlikely to be preoccupied with the critical challenges of the broader society.

In a major review of educational performance in South Africa's first decade of democracy, Stellenbosch economist Servaas van der Berg concludes that while 'quantitative educational attainment differentials (years of education) have been substantially reduced (between learners of different races) ... qualitative differentials remain larger'.[2] Problems of quality are acute in mathematics and science. 'Only 4.6 per cent of all matriculants passed Mathematics at the higher grade in 2002 ... just 22 per cent (of matriculants) passed Physical Science.'

Van der Berg's article is devoted to exploring and seeking to understand what produces the poor performance of the school system as a whole (average outcomes) and also what explains the differences between the best- and worst-performing schools. The article explores a range of issues such as funding, class size, educational qualification of teachers, as well as teacher pay.

Van der Berg also explores race as a factor, assigning a school to a race category where more than 70 per cent of learners (in 1977) belong to that race group. As we note throughout this book, understanding what is going on in our country is constantly made difficult by issues of race. What of the schools where no race group constitutes 70 per cent? What if the analysis was done of the race of teachers? Is the attaching of a race label to a school accurate or useful?

When Van der Berg's results are viewed in their totality, his conclusions are important. 'This may imply that, at the margin, resources may only matter conditionally. The policy implication is that additional fiscal resources by themselves may make only a limited contribution to improving educational performance. Better school management is probably most important, while availability of good teachers remains a binding constraint.'[3]

As important as this finding is, the difference between the best and the worst government schools is huge. This difference is lost in the process of averaging education outcomes. In fact, the top 20 per cent of our country's government schools compete well internationally (with the top 20 per cent of other countries). (We should note that in this top 20 per cent whites constitute a minority.)

This top 20 per cent is critical to meeting society's need for education and skills, and provides almost all of the 85,000 pupils who qualified to go to university last year. (The private schools contributed 7,000 or less than 10 per cent.) Of course the challenge is to close the gap between the top 20 per cent and the rest.[4]

Indeed, perhaps we need to think of a baseline for quality where, for example, enough teaching hours happen to enable the skills of reading, writing and numeracy to be acquired; a baseline of teacher competency; a baseline of order and discipline; a baseline of critical facilities such as computer access and access to books. These create a foundation without which quality becomes impossible. But they are no guarantee of quality education.

The idea of universal access suggests that every child, irrespective of race or class or financial means, should have access to at least some level of education. This idea has been incorporated in many 'bills of rights' from the Atlantic Charter, in which the World War Two Allied powers set out their vision of a post-war world, to the UN Charter and many other documents.

To realise this ideal we must first understand what it means. The language of free education has often been used as a shorthand for universal access. However, this is a shorthand that only takes us so far. It raises almost as many questions as it answers.

Free for whom?

Clearly, constructing (and maintaining) school buildings, hiring teachers and providing teaching materials all require financial resources. Essentially these resources can come from only one of two sources: the family or the state.

If 100 per cent of the cost of schooling comes from the state, it will need to be funded from taxes. Whereas income tax is progressive, this is generally only a third of tax revenues. Consumption taxes such as VAT and corporate taxes impose an equal burden on consumers, employers, employees, customers and suppliers.

Closely connected with the question of who should pay for education is the issue of whether education is a public or a private good, i.e. who benefits from education? The individual educated or society as a whole? As with many such either/or debates, this poses a false choice. Education is quite clearly both a private and a public good. Both the individual and society benefit.

In reality both also have to contribute. A consequence of making schooling compulsory to some level is to deny parents access to the economic benefits of the labour of their children, whether in the home, the self-owned business or elsewhere. Transport costs and many of the attendant costs of being at school (uniforms etc.) are seldom paid for by the government.

At the other end of the scale, only the very rich (say top 5 per cent) can afford to pay the complete cost of schooling. But the cost of such rich-only schooling in terms of diversity and the composition of the class is very high.

The path of wisdom surely suggests that both the state and families should devote as much resource to education as they can possibly afford. Provided this resource is used well, the baseline should be achieved, and quality can then be built.

Ideally, state funding should be determined on a per capita basis. Equity demands this. Individual schools can ensure that the pupil composition reflects diversity and social realism through offering poorer parents partial or full exemption. Denying those parents both willing and able to pay school fees will simply reduce not only the resources available to schooling, but also a critical way of ensuring the efficiency of spending.

A group of wise women and men should produce a working definition of education quality to take this debate further. Another group should examine different ways of funding education.

ACTIONS:
THE LEARNING HOME

As noted above, there is both an opportunity and a need for learning to happen in the home. If your home is rich in books and other kinds of information, this will help greatly. Most importantly, parents need to engage their children in an ongoing conversation about the way in which the world works and does not work. They should get to know what is in the heads of their children. Parents are a child's window on the world, one that is simply not available from schools. Does this window exist? Is it possible to see through it? And how often does it get opened?

The original educator was the community's storyteller. Every human being has stories to share. And as happens between generations, the stories should flow both ways.

Other rich sources of information are books, newspapers, television and the Internet.

ACTIONS:

CHOOSING THE RIGHT SCHOOL FOR YOUR CHILD

This side of heaven, no perfect school exists. Every school has some bad teachers. Every school has problems with drugs, sex and violence. In some schools the head teacher is too new. In others the head has long overstayed her or his appropriate term of office. Diversity and resources will challenge all schools.

Choosing a school is not an easy task. Three criteria do seem useful.

The first is school leadership. This will be immediately evident from even a short visit. Whatever the level of facility and resource, is the school clean and orderly? Are the school buildings in good shape? Is the head teacher a strong leadership presence? Is time-keeping and physical order in the school well maintained? Notice boards, libraries and laboratories will tell you not only about the resources available to learners, but how well or badly these resources are used.

The second is the quality of teachers. Quality here means teachers who have chosen this role as their vocation, teachers for whom teaching is both a first choice and a valued and rewarding activity. More than formal education levels or pay, the love of teaching is what sets out the excellent teacher from the mediocre or average. Is this not what most of us have experienced at school?

Parents would be wise not to be overly impressed by flashy facilities, antique courtyards and the like. 'Mr

Chips' teachers – teachers who love what they do – are found in schools at all levels of resource.

An interesting dimension of these first two criteria is what role if any computers and the Internet play in the school. Www.saschools.co.za lists some 750 schools, with a good mixture of public and private, which have developed a school website. Given the role the digital world will play in the lives of today's children, the school website gives you at least some idea of how computer literate the school community is.

The third criterion is what American scholars have termed, when writing about universities, the 'constitution of the class'. Again, it is our common experience that we learn as much from our fellow scholars as we do from our teachers. What kind of class do we want our child to experience? Some may wish for an exclusive religious or cultural experience. Others may view the experience of diversity in race, religion, culture and class as central to being well educated in this new millennium. Again, the greatest diversity is not necessarily found in the richest, most expensive or best-resourced schools. Indeed, good suburban state schools in South Africa probably offer one of the richest diversity experiences to be found anywhere in the world.

A fourth vital factor in choosing the right school is the nature and character of your child. Each child is unique: some bookish, others sporty, some gregarious, some shy. Taking note of this, indeed involving the child in making the choice, is more likely to match the right kid with the right school.

ACTIONS:

MAKING YOUR CHOICE OF SCHOOL WORK

With considerable effort and lots of homework you and your child will have made your choice of school. The next challenge is to make this choice work.

Two challenges in particular suggest themselves.

The first is for the parent to be an active citizen within the school community.

In terms of the 26,000 state or public schools, South Africa has an extraordinarily democratic system of school governance in which parents have a very high degree of power. Each of these schools must elect regularly a governing body comprising parents of present learners, educators, support staff and learners.

In terms of section 20, chapter 3 of the Schools Act this governing body needs to (amongst other things) adopt its own constitution, develop a mission statement for the school, adopt a code of conduct, determine the timing of the school day, administer the school's property (including buildings) and recommend the appointment of both educators and support staff.

Where these governing bodies are fully functional they can obtain additional powers, in terms of section 21, to maintain and improve buildings and facilities, determine subject choice and extra-curricular activities, purchase books and materials, pay for school services, and conduct adult education and other forms of training.

The governing body is often assisted by a parents'

association, active in mobilising and applying resources to maintaining and expanding the school's effectiveness.

The activism of parents, achieving the needed quorum for electing the governing body, electing people of energy and competence to that body, supporting the governing body in the effective execution of its functions, will determine how well or badly these extensive powers are used. In general, the effectiveness of the governing body is at least as important as the activities of either the provincial or national education department.

A second key role in making the school work for your child is the role of the parent educator. The learner actively acquires an education. It cannot be passively given. Teachers, classrooms, a curriculum, project work: all of these can present opportunities for your child to acquire knowledge, to develop a sense of how things work, to engage the world and find out both how and why it works as it does.

If the child does not engage, then real learning, that development of specific skills (reading, writing, numeracy), competency (critical thinking) and values (life and social skills) just will not happen. Let us return to the words of Ivan Illich quoted at the start of this chapter. When he reflected on how children gain language, he noted that the child acquires this language skill faster 'where the parent pays attention to the child'.

If real learning requires an engaged student, it also needs an engaged parent. This goes a little beyond seeing that the child gets to school on time, and signing the homework book (both very desirable). It involves the parent engaging the child on his learning journey: asking what transpired in the school day, what went well, what went badly; developing some knowledge of the subjects the child likes or hates, and why.

Indeed, the relationship between child and parent is central to effective learning taking place. The productive relationship needed extends much beyond the role of taxi-driver and homework policeman. A learning partnership is needed. It is a partnership because each one has some teaching to offer.

As any good teacher will recognise, the best learner is also a teacher. Those students who participate actively in classroom debate, play leadership roles in cultural and sporting team activities, and bring new knowledge through project work and play into the classroom, are part of collective teaching.

Let us return to Ivan Illich for an instructive story in this regard:

'In 1956 there arose a need to teach Spanish quickly to several hundred teachers, social workers and ministers from the New York Archdiocese so that they could communicate with Puerto Ricans. My friend Gerry Morris announced over a Spanish radio station that he needed native speakers from Harlem. Next day some two hundred teenagers lined up in front of his office, and he selected four dozen of them – many of them school dropouts. He trained them in the use of the US Foreign Service Institute Spanish manual, designed for use by linguists with graduate training, and within a week his teachers were on their own – each in charge of four New Yorkers who wanted to speak the language. Within six months the mission was accomplished. Cardinal Spellman could claim that he had 127 parishes in which at least three staff members could communicate in Spanish.'[5]

ACTIONS:
THE SCHOOL AS A COMMUNITY RESOURCE

Citizens should see the school as a resource both for and from the community. There is much that the community can do for the school. Parents who cannot afford school fees in money can contribute in sweat equity, in teaching, supervising, ensuring safety, and helping with the maintenance of buildings and facilities. The community can offer safe and affordable housing to teachers.

There is equally much the school can offer the community. Learners can also teach as noted above. Why should not almost every school offer adult basic literacy? The school can be a source of economic activity. Many rural schools have food gardens (perhaps something that everyone will need in the future). Schools can run school-feeding schemes, providing markets to local food producers and employment to food providers. Where computing facilities exist, a well-managed school could make these facilities available to the community and earn the school some money.

All of these activities, provided they are properly managed, will enhance both the resources of the school and its teaching mission.

AIDS

'The single most devastating episode in South Africa's demographic history.'

– Professor Howard Phillips, describing the Spanish flu epidemic in South Africa in 1918, in which half a million people are estimated to have died (7 per cent of the total population), making South Africa the fifth hardest-hit country in the worldwide epidemic.

Today our country faces an even greater epidemic, with the country (and region) having one of the highest rate of infection of HIV/AIDS in the world.

IDEAS:

WHAT WE KNOW ABOUT AIDS

The acquired immunodeficiency syndrome (AIDS) is caused by the human immunodeficiency virus. Viruses are parasitic and replicate by entering host cells. The

HIV virus invades cells within the body, and reproduces itself through converting its own ribonucleic acid (RNA) into DNA in the cell, and then converting this DNA back into RNA HIV copies. This multiplying HIV material attacks the cells of the body's immune system, particularly the CD4 cells. Once inside this cell, the virus becomes part of the immune system and is protected from the body's defensive response.

This disease has a very long acting (or developing) time-line. Infected persons may continue without illness for long periods. The progression from the stages described below can vary significantly in time. As the disease involves the progressive failure of the body's immune system, the progression is measured firstly by the decline in the immune system's 'troops', the CD4 cells. A normal CD4 count would be over 1,000 cells per mm^3 of blood.

The World Health Organisation recognises four stages of disease progression.

In *Stage One* of the disease, the patient presents no symptoms. Such a patient will have a CD4 cell count normally greater than 500 per mm^3 of blood.

Symptoms in *Stage Two* are commonly mild weight loss, fungal infections and shingles. Typically the CD4 cell count is between 350 and 500.

In *Stage Three* the patient's immune system is severely suppressed, and symptoms include severe weight loss, diarrhoea and possibly tuberculosis.

In the final stage, *Stage Four*, the CD4 cell count will typically have dropped below 200, and severe illness will now occur including pneumonias and widespread TB.

The first cases are believed to have occurred in the 1930s. AIDS was identified by Atlanta's Center for Disease Control in 1981.

IDEAS:

DIFFERENT PATTERNS OF AIDS IN DIFFERENT PARTS OF THE WORLD

In North America and much of Europe the epidemic was initially focused in homosexual communities. In Eastern Europe, Russia and the former Soviet Union the predominant pattern of spread appears to be through intravenous drug users. In India and China transmission appears to be mainly through contaminated blood.

In sub-Saharan Africa transmission is mainly through heterosexual sex. According to the most recent UNAIDS report (2006), two-thirds of the world's nearly 40 million infected people (or 24.5 million) are to be found in sub-Saharan Africa, followed by Asia with 8.3 million, North America, Western and Central Europe with 2 million, Latin America with 1.6 million, and Eastern Europe and Central Asia with 1.5 million.

Though the evidence is somewhat uneven, not only is the highest concentration of infected persons to be found in sub-Saharan Africa, but the epidemic's increase has been most relentless in this region. The pattern of transmission also affects the widest population groups (in essence all sexually active males and females), as opposed to defined sub-populations such as homosexuals, intravenous drug users, and those infected through blood transfusions. This raises the central question: why?

The virus sub-type prevalent in sub-Saharan Africa
The HIV virus has two major sub-types, known as HIV-1 and HIV-2. The first type is easier to transmit and more fast-acting than the second. It is (mainly) the first virus type that is found in our region.

Poverty

Many have argued that HIV/AIDS is a disease of poverty. However, neither the evidence nor the logic of this disease makes this argument compelling.

'HIV prevalence is not disproportionately higher among poorer adults in sub-Saharan Africa. Indeed in all countries, except Ghana, the trend is the wealthier the person, the more likely they are to be HIV positive.'[1]

At the level of national comparison, two of Africa's richest countries, Botswana and South Africa, have the highest prevalence rates.

What is certainly true is that the impact of HIV/AIDS falls most terribly on the poor, in terms of the rate of advance of the disease, access to treatment, the burden of care, loss of income, etc.

Migrant workers/ truckers/ sex workers

Early in the epidemic, commentators identified high-risk behaviour groups and suggested that not only were they likely to be most infected, but also important transmitters of the disease. Again the evidence does not support this. The South African mining industry, where a high level of migrancy continues, has probably seen more HIV testing than any other South African industry. Prevalence rates have generally placed the industry in the middle of the nine geographic provinces, and significantly behind KwaZulu-Natal, a province with very limited exposure to migrancy.

Though sex workers (and their clients such as truckers) are very logical high-risk behaviour groups, they have proved to be groups in which condom-based prevention strategies have been effective, as the experience of Thailand demonstrates.

Patterns of sexual behaviour

This area of debate is beginning to produce some rather compelling analysis. The debate is of course highly morally charged. Evidence suggests that human sexual behaviour is relatively similar across cultures. The frequency of sex and the number of partners do not appear to differ dramatically between continents. The Victorian notion that sex should only occur in life-long and monogamous marriage, seems more the exception than the rule, everywhere, probably including Victorian

England. Often marriage only loosely regulates sexual relations.

Where patterns of sexual behaviour do seem distinctive in sub-Saharan Africa (and perhaps in the non-Islamic part of this region) is in the prevalence of what epidemiologist and journalist Helen Epstein has called 'long-term concurrency' sexual networks. In such networks individual members have long-term and recurrent sexual relations with several members of the network at the same time in a way that, in epidemiological terms, links each individual with all the others.

In such concurrent (and long-term) networks of sexual relationships, the introduction of safe sex practices such as condoms is as difficult as its introduction into an already established marriage relationship. The sex partners know each other, and have relationships beyond those of sex. Demanding condom use undermines trust, and introduces a changed behaviour that is not easy to explain. This stands in stark contrast to the use of condoms in casual and one-off sex, where issues such as trust and relationship do not feature.

Given that multiple relationships exist inside this network, the introduction of a single infected person is likely to spread the virus much more rapidly than in one-off and single relationships. HIV-positive individuals are the most potent transmitters of the virus in the first month to six weeks after they themselves are infected.

IDEAS:

RESPONDING TO THE AIDS PANDEMIC

Broadly, three strategies have characterised the efforts of society to limit, reduce and stop the spread of the virus.

Information/education campaigns

A good example of such a campaign is the pamphlet distributed to every household in Britain, entitled *AIDS: Don't Die of Ignorance.* In South Africa a very large public awareness campaign has run for many years now under the brand *loveLife.*

These campaigns seek to make citizens aware of the nature of the virus, how it is transmitted, and how it can be avoided.

A number of studies have suggested considerable success in spreading knowledge about HIV and AIDS. In the sub-Saharan context, avoiding becoming infected requires people to organise their sex life in particular ways. These desired behaviours are often presented as the ABC of AIDS prevention: abstain, be faithful and condomise. The evidence suggests that knowledge alone is not very effective in changing patterns of sexual activity. The shift from unprotected to protected sex, for example, requires the male partner's acquiescence. It also introduces the possibility of one or both partners being 'unsafe', as a result of their sexual behaviour outside this particular relationship. It also requires a lot of rationality about one of the least rational aspects of human experience.

Testing HIV status

A second set of strategies involves persuading people to test for their HIV status. This is clearly highly desirable both for the individual and also for potential future sex partners.

Where energy, effort and leadership are applied, considerable success can be achieved, as is indicated in a number of South African mines that have been able to persuade 100 per cent of their workforce to test their status each year. The availability of ARV treatment (see below) gives a powerful incentive to the individual to know his status, and the test should lead to involvement in some health monitoring scheme, where ARV drugs can be made available when the CD cell count indicates this is appropriate. The effective use of ARV therapies has produced great improvements in the state of health of HIV-positive people.

Testing, however, will only reduce the spread of the disease when the HIV-positive person changes his or her patterns of sexual behaviour. Where people are prepared to reveal their status, this clearly empowers potential future sexual partners. This appears, though, rarely to be the case.

The only alternative to relying on voluntary disclosure and behaviour change would be to segregate those who test positive for the disease. One country that has done this is Cuba.

'In the 1980s, the [Cuban] authorities [compulsorily] tested the entire population, isolating those found to be HIV positive in "sanatoria". They continued testing returning migrants. At the end of 2005, there were only about 4,200 infected Cubans.'[2]

In all countries such compulsory testing and social segregation pose serious issues with regard to human rights. In countries which already have a high incidence of disease, given the long periods of gestation of the disease, and indeed its long 'life cycle', huge practical issues also arise for any country wanting to follow the Cuban example.

Vaccines, treatment, and cures

A third group of actions relates to what to do with people who have been infected by the virus. The search for vaccines and cures has been long and intensive. The HIV virus is proving very difficult to combat through either.

'In 2007, there were just four pharmaceutical companies with vaccine trials; only one candidate has gone through all the processes and it was not effective.'[3]

This leads to the conclusion that there will almost certainly not be a vaccine available by 2015.

The major medical breakthrough that has occurred has been the development of the ART drugs. This drug therapy, though not a cure, stabilises and even restores levels of immune resistance and reduces the viral load of the disease. It has given long periods of effective health to many thousands of its users.

This therapy was announced in 1996 and, in the rich and developed part of our world, quickly became a standard treatment for those HIV-positive patients whose CD4 count had deteriorated to a certain level.

This treatment response is being made available in developing countries to increasing numbers of infected persons. Two major hurdles are slowing down this roll-out.

The first is a financial cost. Though the cost of ART drugs has fallen dramatically, current costs suggest that it requires between 54 and 82 US cents per day to keep a person on this treatment. In a world where one in six people live on less than $1 per day, and where government healthcare expenditure is 7 cents a day in Lesotho, and 11 cents in the Ukraine, this is a tough call. Very significant funding from the US President Fund and the Global Fund has made the roll-out possible where local resources could not. But for how long will this donor funding be sustained, given that the ART drugs require to be taken for life?

The second is that ARV treatment requires a well-functioning healthcare system. Patient response to drug therapy needs to be monitored, and both CD4 counts and viral load counts need to be taken. The patient will need regular contact with a healthcare professional. In developing countries many healthcare systems are uneven, and offer very limited access to the poor and those living far from urban centres.

ACTIONS:

BEING OPEN AND HONEST ABOUT HIV AND AIDS

Firstly, the citizen should demand an honest, open debate about this plague. Like all plagues, it flourishes in the dark, in denial, in disguise. Enough is known about the virus that every citizen should be clear about how it is caused, how it is transmitted, how it cannot (for now) be cured, though health can be restored and life extended.

In our part of the world HIV and AIDS combines sex, disease and death. This is a potent combination. Jonny Steinberg has captured the strength of the social taboos in his book *Three Letter Plague,* which describes a sharp, successful young entrepreneur in a village in the Lusikisiki district who refuses to take an HIV test. For as long as this taboo is present, HIV will flourish. And for honesty to prevail people have to be ready not only to test, but also to acknowledge their status openly, and be accepted in the community where they are HIV-positive.

For this to happen the community's leaders will have to lead. This means local politicians, priests, pastors, rabbis and imams. It also means heads of schools (and indeed all teachers), superintendents of hospitals, mayors, chiefs and headmen. It means the leaders of youth and women's organisations, of stokvels and burial societies.

The leadership required is one that both allows and requires those infected with HIV to come out into the light of day. Leadership is needed from the 'top' of society, and also at the 'bottom' in individual communities, and indeed starting with the affected individual himself or herself.

In this regard we have been living with a contradiction. We encourage people to test but promise that the result of their test will be kept confidential. Perhaps this is a valid strategy in a very large city like New York or San Francisco, where people have many options with regard both to testing and to medical care. In most parts of South Africa it is entirely unrealistic. Those that test positive need to join wellness clinics, and attend regularly to have their CD4 counts and viral loads monitored, and when they enter ART treatment regimes to monitor patient response, and receive their medication on a regular basis. In the vast majority of cases this cannot be done without the knowledge, care and support of family, neighbours and workmates.

It is only when HIV-positive people know that they will not be shunned or worse in their community that they will have the courage to live with the disease openly.

We also need open and honest debates about how HIV is transmitted between sexual partners, within families, within communities, and the country and region at large.

The case for very rapid infection in long-term concurrent sex networks is compelling. If this is the way people organise their sexual relationships, any unprotected sex is playing Russian roulette with a fully loaded chamber of bullets.

The evidence of actions which limit transmission also needs to be part of this debate. A number of studies have indicated that circumcised males are significantly less likely to contract the virus.[4]

Circumcision is a sensitive issue in most cultures. In many religious and cultural traditions dietary and health conventions arise in response to specific challenges. We face such a challenge now. We need to create a culture of neonatal medical circumcision, and encourage the practice in adults as well.

Uganda has achieved very significant declines in its HIV prevalence rates. Whilst the causes are much debated, almost certainly delaying the first sexual encounter amongst young girls by one or two years appears to reduce the chance of becoming infected very significantly.

ACTIONS:
RESPONSIBLE SEXUAL BEHAVIOUR

In our part of the world HIV and AIDS is a behavioural disease – that is, it results from the choices we make about our sexual behaviour. Unlike flu or TB, it is not spread through the air. Each citizen who does not wish to be infected, or infect others, must either have sex only with those whose sex history is 'safe', i.e. one partner over a long period of time, or they must not have unprotected sex. It is as straightforward as this.

ACTIONS:
COMPASSION AND INCLUSION

Millions of South Africans are living with HIV or AIDS. They are a vital, functioning part of our community. They are also part of the community living with a real or feared burden of disease, and facing the prospect of death, or having to adhere to unpleasant treatment regimens. We cannot, like Cuba, isolate them. We must include, support and indeed embrace them. This goes beyond the response required of responsible citizens towards those who are HIV-positive or AIDS sick. The AIDS epidemic is reshaping the demography of South Africa, changing life spans, altering age patterns, and leaving a trail of child-headed homes and a generation of orphans. A British scientist, Roy Anderson, has estimated that the course of the epidemic will take 130 years to work its way through the global population. Individuals, families, communities and governments will need to reshape their patterns of care and support in the light of the new architecture of AIDS.

This will not be the first (or the last) challenge to the value set of South Africans. Can we understand AIDS clearly, order our actions in accordance with that knowledge, and reach out to those infected with AIDS?

THE ENVIRONMENT

The citizen in the 21st century faces two major, and thoroughly related, environmental challenges: the first is the world's growing population; the second is global warming.

The world population, according to UN estimates, reached 6 billion in 1999. 'World population did not reach one billion until 1804. It took 123 years to reach 2 billion in 1927, 33 years to reach 3 billion in 1960, 14 years to reach 4 billion in 1974 and 13 years to reach 5 billion in 1987.'[1]

UN projections suggest that the global population will stabilise at around 10 billion people after 2200.

In our continent the population of Africa has grown from around 100 million in 1750 to 900 million today, and is projected to reach 2.4 billion by 2150.

This dramatic growth in the occupants of planet Earth has been made possible through revolutions in agriculture, habitat and hygiene and medical science. All of these are to be celebrated. However, the growing world population is making increasing demands on living space, energy and food consumption.

Three impacts in particular merit our attention. The first is energy. The three major sources of energy today are oil, natural gas and coal.

In inflation-adjusted (i.e. constant money) terms, crude oil prices traded in a narrow range of $18 to $24 per barrel from 1953 to 1973. In the decade of the mid-1970s to mid-1980s they rose to nearly $100. From 1986 to 2003 the price returned to a band between $25 and $35. From 2004 to today prices have risen dramatically to trade at about $130.

Natural gas prices are trading at an all-time high and have risen by 30 per cent this year.

Coal used to generate electricity has seen price rises of some 35 per cent since 2001 in the United States.

The challenge of energy is not only one of radical re-pricing. Actual shortages are being experienced in countries around the world, with rolling blackouts in California and Scandinavia, and energy rationing in Brazil, and of course rolling blackouts and power cuts in South Africa.

The world is also currently in the grip of what the *Washington Post* of 27 April 2008 has described as 'the worst food crisis in a generation', with food prices increasing by 80 per cent between 2005 and early 2008. As with energy, the problem extends beyond pricing. Actual shortages have seen food-related violence, hoarding and export bans in a number of countries around the world. Both rising prices and shortages have a range of causes, from the multi-year drought in Australia, to the use of corn for biofuels, to changing diet in many developing countries.

The third critical area of environmental challenge is that of water. Currently one in six of the world's population lack access to clean drinking water. Water consumption varies very dramatically between the developed and developing world, with average consumption in North America and Japan being around 350 litres per day, compared to 200 in Europe and between 10 and 20 litres in sub-Saharan Africa. With the world's population projected to increase by between 40 and 50 per cent over the next 50 years, water shortages will become acute in many societies.

Global warming

The impact of changed land-use, the burning of fossil fuels and other patterns of human activity are contributing to a second major environmental challenge: that of global warming.

Since the advent of reliable data collection in 1850, average global temperatures have risen by close to 1°C.[2] The largest collective scientific investigation into climate change, involving 2,500 scientists, 174 lead authors and 222 contributing authors, the United Nations-convened Intergovernmental Panel on Climate Change (www.ipcc. ch), has estimated in its fourth report, released in 2007, that average temperatures are likely to rise by a further 3°C over the next century, and that such warming will cause rising sea levels, stronger storms and hurricanes, shifting rainfall patterns, increasing floods, droughts and famines, and mass migrations from the worst-affected areas. This UN study concluded that there was a 90 per cent certainty that warming was 'in large part caused by human actions such as deforestation and the burning of fossil fuels'. A major focus of continuing scientific inquiry is the extent, rate and consequence of the melting of polar ice-caps.

Though the pattern of warming is generally agreed, its causes remain disputed, and more importantly the appropriate response from both developed and developing nations remains deeply debated. Environmentalist sceptics strongly suggest that resources should be focused on combating tuberculosis and malaria, and preventing conflict.

A new world treaty, replacing the Kyoto Protocol, on responding to global warming will be negotiated at a conference in Copenhagen in 2009.

IDEAS: ELECTRICITY
WHAT WENT WRONG?

Whilst finger-pointing and blaming achieve little, it is important to understand what caused South Africa's energy crisis which closed the South African mining industry for five days in January 2008 for the first time since the Anglo-Boer War, saw at first unplanned and then planned outages across the country, and has hit both economic activity and the confidence of our citizenry.

A small group of independent, appropriately experienced and skilled individuals should be tasked to review what led to this crisis and what we need to do to avoid a recurrence.

IDEAS:
ENERGY EFFICIENCY

The South African public needs a clear understanding of the efficient use of energy in lighting and heating, as well as in other applications. An expert and independent body like the CSIR should be charged with setting energy-efficiency standards that citizens could use to benchmark their own use of energy.

IDEAS:
ALTERNATIVE SOURCES OF ENERGY

Again, either an expert panel or some expert body needs to give clear information about the cost and realistic possibilities of supply (how much and how long) of solar, wind, and nuclear energy sources.

IDEAS:
BOOSTING FOOD PRODUCTION IN SOUTH AFRICA

How well or badly have we done in raising yields and

increasing the production of key foodstuffs in our country? What is the relative contribution of large-scale commercial farming and small-scale farmers? What is the extent and effectiveness of agricultural support services? How much is South Africa spending on agricultural research, and in particular on improving seeds? What are the issues around genetically modified foods, and what should our national policy be on this issue?

IDEAS:
DEVELOPING A REGIONAL FOOD MARKET

South Africa is a country with limited agriculturally useful land. Many other parts of our region have better rainfall and more productive land. Could we fast-track open markets in food production in the southern African region?

IDEAS:
DEVELOPING REGIONAL WATER MARKETS

South Africa is a water-scarce country. Other parts of our region are at least relatively water-rich. A regional panel should develop a southern African water strategy, which regional investment could make a reality.

IDEAS: GLOBAL WARMING
UNDERSTANDING THE REGIONAL AND NATIONAL LIKELY IMPACTS

If temperatures do rise by 3 degrees over the next century, what are the likely impacts on our country and region? The effects will be uneven. What can we do to reduce at least the worst impact of these effects? And how can we benefit from the positive effects?

IDEAS: GLOBAL WARMING
GETTING READY FOR COPENHAGEN

Can the developing world agree on a strategy for a new Kyoto Accord?

So far the debate has been undermined by an arrogance in attitude from developed countries, and a corresponding (and equally unhelpful) defiance on the part of the developing world.

Often the developed world speaks in a language that quite overlooks their own history, as well as their current dominance in the use of resources. Developing countries face the challenge of development. Often this involves extending access to energy, water and a richer diet to millions of their people. Developed countries are the greatest users (and, many would argue, abusers) of these scarce resources, whose use appears to be a direct cause of global warming.

But the developed and developing world share

one small planet. Rising temperatures, higher oceans and changed rainfall will affect both rich and poor nations alike. Both need to be ready to make sacrifices if the worst possibilities of global warming are to be avoided.

What is needed is behaviour change in both categories of countries, as well as smart partnerships whereby the use of best technologies allows developing nations to extend access without matching developed nations' per capita usages.

Can South Africa help facilitate such an agreement? What do South Africans want for a new Kyoto Accord?

ACTIONS: ENERGY
THE TEN PER CENT CLUB

The national energy grid is operating on a margin between supply and demand of between 5 and 7 per cent. This means that any significant interruption in one of the country's power stations, or any significant problem in any part of the national distribution grid, is likely to force electricity outages.

In the extreme situation where demand consumes the level of power needed to maintain the grid itself, the country could face a national blackout lasting weeks.

A range of short-, medium- and long-term actions are under way to restore the margin to a more acceptable level of around 19 per cent. However, there is only one reliable way to prevent sporadic or general power outages. This is for every electricity user to use less. The country is aiming to achieve a 10 per cent saving in both peak (at a moment in time) and total (over a period of time) demand.

Citizens can join the ten per cent club, being the club of people who are regularly achieving the desired saving. The first step is to know your current level of use. This is readily available on a monthly basis through the bill for electricity. It is available daily (indeed hourly) for all users who have meters.

Just a few actions can result in major savings. The biggest win by far is to replace electricity-fuelled water geysers with solar geysers. South Africa boasts one of the highest levels of sunlight in the world. Solar geysers are effective. They involve a big upfront cost (geysers and installation range from R11,000 to around R30,000). Subsidies are available. At current and likely future prices the pay-back period will be very quick.

Installing energy-efficient light bulbs is the next big win.

Citizens who can diversify their sources of energy, for example by using gas for cooking and heating, will also easily meet the 10 per cent goal.

Industry, commerce and public administration all need to achieve the 10 per cent reduction. But citizens in their homes consume 40 per cent of electricity usage. If we can do it, the national grid will be halfway there.

Reduced usage now is the only sure way to keep the lights on. It carries a benefit beyond the avoidance of blackouts. It will also reduce the electricity bill, leaving a little more cash to meet the mountain of other demands. It also reduces the levels of fossil-fuel burning and helps reduce the country's carbon footprint.

ACTIONS:
TRANSPORT

It is not only electricity whose price is increasing rapidly. The price of petrol and diesel has gone through the roof. In January 2002 petrol in Gauteng cost R3.66 a litre, and diesel R3.40 a litre. Today unleaded 95 petrol is R9.83 a litre, and diesel R10.85. Some shortages have been experienced in supply, and the supply situation for diesel in the interior may become critical as one of the pipelines undergoes maintenance.

Every reason therefore exists to use this fuel both more effectively and less.

As with electricity the best way of saving is to drive less. Going to and from work is the form of transport most people use most frequently. Using public transport or car-sharing will most dramatically cut back your petrol bill.

When you are driving your own car, checking oil and tyre pressure will help keep petrol consumption as effective as possible. Planning routes and driving at controlled and even speeds will also achieve this.

ACTIONS:

FOOD

As with most issues discussed in this book, the deliberate planning of how you want to eat offers the best chance to get the best value for the money you spend. Often there will be a trade-off between the time spent planning (and shopping) and the value achieved. Often a shorter food cycle, i.e. planning and buying food for a week or even a few days rather than a month, will allow you to match what is available (for good value) and what you want to eat. Convenience foods are very often both wasteful and unhealthy.

The richer parts of the world (and the richer parts of our society) waste an astonishing amount of food. Tim Jones from the University of Arizona found after a ten-year study that the US household threw out about $50 billion worth of food each year. You can easily check your own wastage 'margin' by keeping food waste separate from other waste for just one week (or even one day). To reduce food waste you need to determine why you are throwing things away. Common reasons are purchases in too large quantities; 'wrong' purchases (Johnny loves …); meal portions that are too large; poor storage (plastic storage containers pretty soon pay for themselves).

South Africa is too rich a country for people to go to bed hungry. Each of us who has the means to put food on the family table also has a responsibility to make food available to the destitute. Many religious organisations already operate food centres. Surely each member of the congregation could contribute some food at each weekly service?

ACTIONS:
WATER

Water, like energy and food, is both scarce, and constantly becoming more expensive. There is no reason why most citizens cannot reduce their consumption of water by 10 per cent. As with the other two resources a few simple actions should achieve a saving of this magnitude. First, attend to leaks quickly. Second, use toilet, bath, shower, washing machines and dishwashers efficiently. Reduce the flush of the toilet either by a half-flush device or simply a brick or bag put into the cistern. Showers use much less water than baths. Water-based household devices such as washing machines and dishwashers should be used for full loads only. Third, those living in areas with at least periods of extensive rain should consider installing a rain tank to collect rainwater.

ACTIONS:
GLOBAL WARMING

The active and responsible citizen will make his or her use of our small planet's natural resources deliberate, planned and efficient. And less! Perhaps we need a ten per cent less club for all three areas of resource: energy, food and water. Almost certainly we will be well on the way to a better relationship between our world and ourselves.

THE FAMILY

'In a permanently unsettled world like ours, no other form of living together can replace the practical resources this type of family has to offer modern individuals.'
– Brigitte Berger[1]

The home is a citizen's castle, as the old English saying goes. It is where she or he spends most time. It is the immediate society in which the citizen acts out his or her most important roles.

THE FAMILY IN GLOBAL CONTEXT

In her book *The Family in the Modern Age* the American sociologist Brigitte Berger notes that across both time and cultures many different types of family have existed. Ethnographers have identified six key characteristics common to all:

rules for organising sexual conduct;
patterns for producing and protecting children;
rules for the rights and duties of marriage partners

and children;
shared living arrangements;
rules for the economic obligations of partners
and towards children;
rules for descendants and inheritance.

Beyond the six characteristics Berger describes the family in the following ways:

'The family ... is the product of the most elementary and the most virulent emotions of human nature – love, hate, sex, hunger, sacrifice, punishment, loneliness, and so on.'[2]

What do we mean by the modern, nuclear family? We mean a family/household set up through the mutual consent of two people, in which they and their children live together.

In pre-industrial societies the vast majority of people were dependent on a chief, lord, squire or local ruler for a place to live. Their economic activity was determined by what was known as their station in traditional society. Marriage was arranged. Generally, in such societies women occupied positions of low power and bore most of the economic burden of existence. Children had many duties and not many rights. Social mobility and individual choice were virtually non-existent.

New patterns of economic activity, and particularly the separation of 'work' from the land and those who controlled it, created spaces in which the young could seek economic independence, choose a life partner and set up their own household.

'Modern society requires individuals to develop a distinctive sense of time and space, a capacity for self reliance, motivation, achievement, collaboration and sharing, habits of trust and inquisitiveness, just to mention some of the behavioural ingredients important … in the complex networks of the modern world.'[3]

We have argued in the chapter on education that a 'learning home' and a 'teaching parent' are essential foundations for a good education. But the family's role is much broader than this. As the quote suggests, it is a factory of the new social order both created by and needed for modern, urban society.

The home and household is where children first learn language, manners, a concept of time and 'reciprocity', i.e. how you negotiate with someone else for what you want. They learn about money and responsibilities. In fact they encounter society.

The family: a resource for the poor

Some have written about the modern, nuclear family as if it was an exclusively middle-class structure. This is simply a product of their own social reality and limited resource. For the newly urbanising poor, and even more those who cross national boundaries in search of work and opportunity, the family is a vital resource. It is at least a source of shared expense, and often the base for economic activity. Often the family household is literally what allows the individual to survive in a harsh new environment.[4]

The family in the South African context

South Africa shared a colonial history with the rest of the African, South American and Asian continents in the last centuries of the previous millennium. This had the effect of making the transition from traditional, agrarian societies to industrial or proto-industrial societies abrupt, brutal and incomplete. The policies of racial separation and minority rule further distorted this transition. Migratory labour became a permanent pattern rather than a process of transition. Restricted access to land, capital and skills confined black South Africans to poverty ghettos in the new urban and industrial order. A radically unequal access to both state and social resources ensured that black South Africans had the poorest education, health and housing resources.[5]

These then were some of the challenges confronting South Africa's first non-racial, democratic government when it assumed power in April 1994.

Fourteen years later the social context of the South African family is as follows: 56 per cent of the population live in urban areas. Of a population of 48 million, 30 million are of working age (15 to 65 years). Of these some 13 million are in employment, with a further 4 million unemployed.

Researchers have noted that in the African continent, marriage 'is generally universal, early and characterised by low divorce rates'.[6] South Africans, in contrast, marry comparatively late, with the average age of first marriage for males 30.5 years, and for females 27.7 years.[7] Some 49 per cent of those 15 years and older have never married. However, this average is the result of very high not-married levels in the earlier age groups:

15-19: *99 per cent;*
20-24: *92 per cent;*
25-29: *70 per cent.*

Consistent with the late marrying pattern, it falls dramatically after 30:

30-34: *45 per cent;*
35-39: *29 per cent;*
40-44: *21 per cent;*
45-49: *15 per cent;*
50+:   *10 per cent.*[8]

In the period 1997 to 2006 the annual number of registered marriages rose by 26 per cent to 184,860. Over the same period the number of divorces declined from 37,098 to 31,270. Of these divorces 60 per cent involved marriages with children.[9]

In an attempt to address the challenges of poverty, child support and old age, the state pays social grants to the elderly, and to those responsible for supporting children, including foster children. Currently some 11 million South Africans are receiving such grants.

In this context the family faces some very specific threats.

Firstly, the AIDS plague is radically altering the 'normal' family structure. There are large numbers of child-headed households, and family structures have been changed through parental death and informal adoption of surviving children.

Secondly, widespread and chronic unemployment has altered the economic structure of the household, with the only income now often coming from an elderly parent or unmarried or unattached mother.

Thirdly, an absence of economic opportunity in rural South Africa has caused many to leave communal (tribal) lands to seek a better fortune in South Africa's towns and cities. However, a severe shortage of formal housing sees many competing for space in informal settlements. When an influx of foreigners, very probably numbering in the millions, is added to this mix, xenophobic violence is not very surprising.

Not only is formal housing in short supply, it is also very expensive. Over the last two decades very little has been added to South Africa's stock of rental residential accommodation. The last five years or so have seen a significant increase in house prices (though these are now flat and falling). Combined with interest rate hikes this has made mortgage repayments onerous for all, and impossible for a growing number of homeowners.

After work and housing, probably the next priority for many households is good education for children. Many enterprising families in working-class areas have organised for their children to attend good suburban or rural schools, at considerable cost. In many parts of our country township schools stand empty.

The urban poor in South Africa generally live far

from the places where work opportunities might be found. Public transport is poor, dominated by mini-bus taxis, which are unsubsidised.

Against this bleak background the survival of families is testimony to their resourcefulness, and to the support they draw from many elements of civil society.

If it is true that the family household is the building block of modern society, then surely it is time for our country to take stock of the challenges faced by the family and look for ways to support it.

IDEAS:

A 'BLUE RIBBON' COMMISSION ON HOW TO BETTER SUPPORT SOUTH AFRICAN FAMILIES

Let us bring together a small group of wise citizens who can think about ways to better support the family. Such a 'blue ribbon' (expert rather than representative) body could be set up by government, or it could be created by civil society. With the right membership it should be equally effective.

As Wikipedia notes, 'the informal term "blue-ribbon" is used to describe a group of exceptional persons appointed to investigate or study a given question. The term generally connotes a degree of independence from political influence or other authority … their value comes from their ability to use their expertise to issue findings or recommendations.' Two recent American examples of such blue ribbon commissions are the 9/11

Commission appointed by President Bush and the Iraq Study Group appointed by the US Congress.

Such a body could examine fiscal support both through tax exemptions and direct grants. They could look at ways of making some form of formal housing more affordable for first-time homeowners. They could examine possible responses to the issues of AIDS orphans, and child-headed households. They should be looking at how government and society can better respond to the needs of this essential building block in our social order.

ACTIONS:
SETTING UP A HOUSEHOLD

Despite the rise of economically independent individuals (particularly women), and more liberal attitudes to sex and childbirth outside marriage, most people around the world aspire to a conventional marriage in the context of the modern, nuclear family. In a 2006 Human Sciences Research Council Survey an average of 87 per cent of all race groups supported marriage to one partner throughout one's life.

Increasingly world-wide, and overwhelmingly in South Africa, the individual not only chooses to marry but also chooses the partner she or he intends to spend the rest of their lives with. This choice is the consequence of love.

This is a big choice, and should be made carefully and

consciously. Whilst the law may allow for dissolution of marriage, a life partner chosen in love and chosen for life should not be easily discarded. The price of such discarding is very high indeed, and more particularly so when children are involved.

ACTIONS:
LOVE AND FREEDOM FOR YOUR PARTNER

If marriage is accepted and lived as a real partnership, each partner should be able to balance his or her role in the family and household with the role she or he performs in broader society. The balance will never be complete or simple. It will involve give and take. And the demands of children will make maintaining a balance between individual freedom and the needs of the family so much harder. But the richness which a partner brings into the partnership, into the marriage and into the home from roles outside it will deepen and strengthen the marriage greatly.

Perhaps a word on gender relations would be useful here. The authors are both married to very strong, independent women. We love these women and especially love their strength and independence. The authors do not believe that men and women are the same. We do believe that men and women are human beings of equal worth and that society should offer both men and women every opportunity to fulfil their dreams. In our experience partnerships in life (inside the family and out) bring together people who have a common goal and who each bring different abilities and energies to the achievement of that goal. It is indeed the different contributions that make the partnership both strong and worthwhile.

Brigitte Berger has described this well:

'Modern men and women have come to realize that the lover who encourages independence in the one he loves, who helps them do their own things, improves the quality of their love and thereby the quality of their life together.'[10]

ACTIONS:

THE ENGAGED PARENT

Raising children in the modern world involves more work, more choice, more effort, and more uncertainty than ever before. This huge social challenge needs to be met in the context in which both parents may well have more conflicting demands on their time than ever.

Two things seem very clear in this regard.

The need for expanded childcare

Firstly, we need to find all sources of support for parents. Access to safe and loving childcare resources, whether in the home, at work or at a crèche, nursery school or after-school facility, is crucial. This is both a critical need and an important opportunity. As the participation of women in the formal economy continues to grow, the demand for childcare will grow with it. It is a challenge for government and society at all levels to ensure that appropriately trained, resourced and funded child-carers are available to meet this need.

Not only will expanding well-trained childcare strengthen the family, it will also create work for many relatively poorly educated individuals.

There is perhaps an expanding opportunity for schools to offer after-care (and sometimes pre-care) facilities as an additional (and separately funded) resource for parents. Perhaps this could be a source of funding for schools, and also a source of money for those parents who have the time to assist with care or transport.

The issue of funding requires further thought. The childcare social grant is a major source of financial support. The grant is certainly an effective way of supporting the poorest parents. There may be additional and more cost-effective ways of supporting childcare for those involved in the formal economy through more substantial tax credits.

The continuing central role of parents

Well-resourced and effectively trained child-carers, grandparents, neighbours, and good schools: all these help to make the job of the parent possible. In the end nobody cares as much about the needs of the child, and nobody knows as much about how to meet those needs, as the parent. The job of parenting can be shared. It can never be outsourced.

The parent remains as important an educator as the best teacher; as vital a doctor as the best GP; as critical a counsellor as the best psychologist.

Especially where both parents are at work (but even where they are not), parenting needs to be a shared responsibility. The burden of single parenting is enormous. To find the energy, wisdom, patience and persistence to meet the challenges of one's child is too much for a single individual.

But this role is not only about duty (though duty is certainly involved). It is also about love, about time and experience shared, about discovering the world through a new pair of eyes.

AN AGENDA FOR A BETTER
SOUTH AFRICA

Politicians and the media generally determine the debate about how to build a better South Africa. Yet citizens are required as both co-architects and co-builders, and it is the citizen who inhabits the house so constructed. Citizens should therefore help to shape this debate. In this book we have looked at a better society in a number of ways. In this concluding chapter we pick up some of the ideas that could get us there. Readers will have their own proposals and we look forward to reading them on the website.

A TOOLKIT FOR A SHARED IDENTITY

Let's agree on a pledge of allegiance, and perhaps a call to action. The words in the constitution are a pretty good start. Let a Committee of Elders propose and let the nation vote at the time of the next general election.

Let's also create a standing Names Commission to propose some national name changes (a package) every five years, and to provide a list of suitable names for provincial and local government.

Let's have a review of the country's national holidays to make the national calendar inclusive. (And why don't we reduce the number of holidays but attach them to weekends?)

BEYOND THE TRIBE, OUTSIDE THE GHETTO

Let us acknowledge South Africa's different tribes, and celebrate their diversity.

Accepting that we all live in ghettos, let us also discover our country outside these ghettos.

Let's act quickly and decisively on xenophobia: tough police and army action against violence; temporary legalisation for those who obey our laws; tough action for those foreigners who break them; and a quick route (three years?) to those who want to become citizens.

CRIME

Crime is a key national priority. Let us mobilise our communities to give criminals no place to hide, including through making tax payments public. Let us create youth activities to start including the large number of inactive young people.

FINDING WORK, MAKING MONEY

Let's get our best national brains to devise a plan for five million more jobs.

MANAGING MONEY, AVOIDING DEBT

Let us set national targets for consumer debt, both for the national economy and for individual households.

Let us extend the National Credit Act to cover credit cards, promote savings and credit unions, and bring the Mashonisa in from the cold.

EDUCATION

Let us set out what quality education means at school level in terms of minimum performance. From this let us understand the human and financial resources schools need to achieve these targets. Then let us design a strategy to achieve access for every child to such quality education drawing on the combined resources of government, parents, the school itself and the community.

AIDS

Let a panel of experts determine why this disease has spread so quickly and so extensively in sub-Saharan Africa. Let civil society lead a campaign of honesty and openness about AIDS so that people can disclose their status.

ENVIRONMENT

We need an expert review to determine what went wrong with our country's electricity supply. Let us unite our nation around the goal of every user of electricity saving at least ten per cent of current use.

Let us design a strategy to boost food consumption, reduce food wastage, and ensure that no South African goes to sleep hungry.

We need an expertly designed national water strategy.

Let South Africa be a lead voice of developing nations at the Copenhagen conference on global warming in 2009.

THE FAMILY

Let an eminent persons' group design a programme to support the family, including child-headed and economically inactive families.

A CHARTER OF THE ACTIONS OF THE ACTIVE, RESPONSIBLE CITIZEN

'I, Dr Thokoana James Motlatsi and Robert Michael Godsell, recognise the injustices of our past; honour those who suffered for justice and freedom; respect those who have worked to build and develop our country; and believe that South Africa belongs to all who live in it, united in diversity.

I am a citizen of this country determined to build a **future** that is **better than our past**. In politics I will be an **active member** of the **political party** I support, help **shape** its **values** and **choose** its **leaders**. Beyond politics and in the places where government has little reach, I will **act** as a **responsible citizen**.

I will help to build a **shared South African national identity**, learning about South Africans different from me; finding common cause across groups; exposing myself to other languages and cultures beyond my **tribe** and outside my **ghetto**.

The high level of **crime** is one of our country's biggest challenges. In my community I will strive to give criminals **no place to hide**. I will **boycott stolen goods**. I will support the crime-busters in my neighbourhood. I will expect of them the highest levels of **training**, decent **employment conditions** and employees **without criminal records** from **private security companies I employ**.

I will use the **resources** and **networks** that I have to **find work** and **make money**.

I will understand the **true cost** of any **debt** and set **personal targets** for **levels** of debt, especially housing debt.

I will make my **home** a **place of learning** for my children. With them we will choose the **right schools**, and make this choice **work**, through being **active members** of the school **community**.

I will be **open** and **honest** about **AIDS**. I will take **full responsibility** for my own sexual conduct and will not endanger the lives of my sex partners. I will be **compassionate** towards fellow citizens with **AIDS**.

I will reduce my use of **electricity** by **ten per cent** and use **petrol** and **water** efficiently. I will reduce **food wastage** and ensure that nobody in my neighbourhood goes to sleep **hungry**.

I will treat my **life partner** with **respect** and **dignity**. I will be an **active** and **engaged parent**.

NOTES

A NATION UNDER CONSTRUCTION

[1] G.H. Calpin, *There are No South Africans*, Thomas Nelson, London, 1941, p. 9.

[2] Nadine Gordimer, *A World of Strangers*, 1958.

[3] A full text of the speech is available on the website www.soweto.co.za.

[4] Nicholas Ostler makes the point that 'Curiously but significantly, it was only in Africa that [the Dutch] colonial intrusiveness bore any linguistic fruit ... Taking all [the South Africans], the 10 million who know the language compare significantly with the 20 million or so who now speak Dutch worldwide.' N. Ostler, *Empires of the Word*, HarperCollins, London, 2005, p. 399.

[5] Thomas Sowell, *Ethnic America*, Basic Books, New York, 1981, p. 3.

[6] Drew Gilpin Faust, *The Republic of Suffering*, Alfred A. Knopf, New York, 2008, p. xi.

[7] Ministry of Education and Training, *Education for Human Rights and Democracy: Teachers' Handbook*, Unesco, Maseru, 2007.

[8] These words are taken almost literally from the preamble to the South African Constitution, adopted into law in 1996.

[9] President Thabo Mbeki speaking on the adoption into law of the South African Constitution, 8 May 1996.

[10] Simon Schama, *Citizens: A Chronicle of the French Revolution*, Penguin, London, 1989.

[11] William Doyle, *The Oxford History of the French Revolution*, Oxford University Press, Oxford, 1989, p. 107.

[12] Ibid.

[13] ANC 2004 website.

BEYOND THE TRIBE, OUTSIDE THE GHETTO
[1] Call for a Commission of Inquiry into May 2008 Violence, Centre for Development and Enterprise, press release, 17 July 2008.

CRIME
[1] Marc Mieroop, *King Hammurabi of Babylon: A Biography*, Blackwell Publishers, Cambridge, 2004.
[2] Sections 11 and 12 of the Bill of Rights, which forms Chapter 2 of our Constitution
[3] 'Crime Situation in South Africa: April–September 2007', Crime Information Analysis Centre, South African Police Service, released December 2007. This detailed (35 page) analysis of crime trends in the period under review is very useful in understanding actual patterns of criminal activity
[4] Economic and Social Council of the United Nations, *Global Report on Crime and Justice*, Oxford University Press, Oxford, 1999.
[5] Ibid.
[6] Alfred Blumstein and Joel Wallman (eds.), *The Crime Drop in America*, Cambridge University Press, Cambridge, 2000, Chapter 9.

FINDING WORK, MAKING MONEY
[1] *Financial Mail*, 26 October 2007, pp. 36–48.
[2] James Kynge, *China Shakes the World: The Rise of a Hungry Nation*, Weidenfeld and Nicolson, London, 2006, p. 9.
[3] Ibid., pp. 16, 20, 21.
[4] Ibid., p. 32.
[5] Ibid., p. 19.
[6] Ibid., p. 19.

MANAGING MONEY, AVOIDING DEBT

[1] Charles Dickens, *David Copperfield*, Penguin, London, 1996, p. 59.

[2] This data is drawn from a *Business Day* report, 28 February 2008, quoting the National Credit Regulator CEO, Gabriel Davel.

[3] 'Credit Extension to Houses', Report prepared for the National Credit Regulator, December 2006, p. 1.

[4] Ibid, page 1.

[5] *Business Day*, 28 February 2008.

[6] We say 'appears' to be, as the applicable interest is not easy to determine from the website-based information on these credit cards. Try for yourself!

EDUCATION

[1] Ivan Illich, *Deschooling Society*, Penguin, Harmondsworth, 1971, p. 20.

[2] S. van der Bergh, 'Apartheid's enduring legacy: inequalities in education', *Journal of African Economy*, 16, 5, August, 2007.

[3]. Ibid., p. 871.

[4] Ibid., p. 875.

[5] Ibid., p. 22.

AIDS

[1] A. Whiteside, *HIV/AIDS: A Very Short Introduction*, Oxford University Press, Oxford, 2008, p. 53.

[2] Ibid., p. 107.

[3] Ibid., p. 111.

[4] Ibid., pp. 37 and 38.

ENVIRONMENT

[1] *The World at Six Billion*, United Nations Publications, New York, 2000, p. 3.

[2] *Financial Times*, supplement, 3 June 2008, pp. 8 and 9.

FAMILY

1 Brigitte Berger, *The Family in Contemporary Times*, 2006, p. 209.

2 Ibid., p. 79.

3 Ibid., p. 87.

4 'Detailed studies on the migratory experience (in Latin America) indicate that the family gains new and added significance in the migrant's encounter with a great variety of urban challenges ... It is of singular importance to note that both small-scale entrepreneurial activities as well as new forms of interaction occur within the context of the family household. The stability of the family relationships that provides the urban poor with a competitive advantage hence becomes vitally important. Bryan Roberts, for instance, found that among the urban poor in Guatemala City many of the family unions were quite stable despite the fact that a large portion of the couples living together were not married by either church or state. Similar findings can be gleaned from studies conducted in Brazil as well as Chile, Peru and Mexico. The harsh economic and social realities of migrant life in the penny economy require new forms of interaction, of trust, of planning, and of looking toward the future. In acquiring such new forms of thought and action in the context of the household economy, the migrants are able to invent not only new modes of being, they also reinvent the family.' (Ibid., pp. 131 and 132)

5 For a fuller description of the impacts of both colonialism and race politics on the evolution of the family, see Chapter 1 of Acheampong Yaw Amoateng and Tim B. Heaton (eds.), *Families and Households in Post-apartheid South Africa: Socio-Demographic Perspectives*, HSRC Press, Cape Town, 2007.

6 Ibid., p. 93..

7 Ibid.

8 Ibid., pp. 100, 101.

9 *Marriages and Divorces, 2006*, Statistics South Africa, Pretoria, December 2007.

10 Berger, *The Family*, p. 173.

SOURCES AND SUGGESTED
FURTHER READING

G.H. Calpin's book *There are No South Africans* (Thomas Nelson, 1941) describes the essential failure of the project to bring together the two Boer Republics and the two English colonies in the Union of South Africa. Black South Africans hardly feature at all in the book.

Nadine Gordimer's *A World of Strangers* (1958) paints a picture of white and black South Africans who inhabit the same country but share almost no part of the country's 'social reality'.

A full copy of Thabo Mbeki's speech *I Am an African* can be found on the following website: www.soweto. co.za/html/i_iamafrican.htm

The Constitution of the Republic of South Africa. In particular, citizens should read the preamble and the Bill of Rights. The full constitution is available in bookshops, and can also be accessed on the website www.info.gov.za/documents/constitution/index.htm

Another book which well describes the ghettos in which South Africans of different races, languages and cultures live is Alan Paton's classic *Cry, the Beloved Country* (1948). It remains a sadly relevant guide to the many worlds which continue to exist within our borders.

On the cover of Nicholas Ostler's *Empires of the Word* (HarperCollins, 2005), a world map is delineated in the words of world languages. Southern African is expressed in Afrikaans, and in the words: 'Alle menslike wesens word vry, met gelyke waardigheid en regte gebore/ Hulle het rede en gewete en behoort in die gees van broederskap teenoor mekaar op te tree.' Good words to put on a map!

In his book *Ethnic America* (Basic Books, 1981), Thomas Sowell traces the peopling of his country, beyond its original inhabitants, through immigration from Europe, Asia, Africa and Latin America. He also explores the consequences of the 'cultural baggage' each group brought with them, quoting another historian who said: 'We do not live in the past, but the past lives in us.' This book is one of the most thoughtful analyses of the social, political and economic impacts of culture.

In Drew Gilpin Faust's *This Republic of Suffering* (Alfred A. Knopf, 2008), the author sets out to record and understand how the memories of the American

Civil War have shaped its subsequent history. It is a good reminder of the truth of William Faulkner's saying, 'The past isn't dead and buried. It isn't even past.' Barack Obama quoted Faulkner in his speech on race relations. The emergence and dramatic popularity of the song *Delarey* amongst Afrikaans-speaking South Africans in these early years of the 21st century is a reminder of this truth at home.

In *Citizens: A Chronicle of the French Revolution* (Penguin Books, 1989), the English historian Simon Schama writes about this seminal event in European history in terms of three themes: 'The first concerns the problematic relationship between patriotism and liberty ... The second ... turns on the 18th century belief that citizenship was, in part, the public expression of an idealized family ... Finally, the book attempts to confront directly the painful problem of revolutionary violence.'

The full text of Barack Obama's speech *Towards a More Perfect Union* is available on the following website: www.nytimes.com/2008/03/18/us/politics/18text-obama.html

Amos Elon's *The Pity of It All: A Portrait of Jews in Germany 1743–1933* (Penguin, 2004) tells the story of the vital role played by this religious community in Germany's history over two centuries.

Jonathan Sacks, Chief Rabbi of Britain, has written a challenging essay entitled *The Dignity of Difference* (Continuum, 2002) on the ways in which cultural, and more particularly religious, differences can become a positive force in diverse societies.

In his book *China Shakes the World: The Rise of a Hungry Nation* (Weidenfeld and Nicolson, 2006), the English journalist James Kynge has written an excellent account of the social and economic changes currently occurring in China, as well as their implications for other countries.

Creating Jobs One by One: A Manual for Enthusiastic Amateurs, by Ian Clark and Gillian Godsell, provides intensely practical advice to those wanting to start their own (small) businesses. Copies available from the authors.

Ivan Illich published his radical (i.e. going to the roots) critique of schools in *Deschooling Society* (Calder and Boyars, 1971).

Alan Whiteside's *HIV/AIDS: A Very Short Introduction* (Oxford University Press, 2008) provides an excellent, short and very readable introduction to this subject.

Jonny Steinberg's *Three-Letter Plague* (Jonathan Ball, 2008) describes the realities of stigma, fear and prejudice which surrounds the HIV/AIDS virus in a deep rural area in the Eastern Cape.

In Helen Epstein's book *The Invisible Cure: Africa, the West and the Fight against AIDS* (Farrar, Straus, 2007) explores patterns of sexual relationships in sub-Saharan Africa and suggests their probable relationship to the very rapid spread of the virus through heterosexual relationships.

Nicolas Stern, economic adviser to the British Government, has provided an encyclopedic review of the economics of climate change and climate change mitigation in his report *The Economics of Climate Change: The Stern Review* (Cambridge University Press, 2008).

Brigitte Berger's *The Family in the Modern Age: More than a Life Style Choice* (Transaction Publishers, 2002) provides rich research data, ideas and analysis about the modern family, setting a useful global context for the South African family.